"From the first page to the last, I re
and sometimes tears in my eyes. I
will experience as they read it—a
one who has both resisted extending forgiveness and needed to be forgiven. While admitting that it might take time and will likely be messy and complex, Wendy makes the miracle of grace required for forgiveness, confession, repentance, and release seem possible. This is the hope we all need to take a step forward."

Nancy Guthrie, Author and Bible Teacher

"This is an honest book. Alsup is not writing an abstract treatise on forgiveness and reconciliation, but has rather interwoven the deeply personal threads of her own story with a profound and extended meditation on the life of Joseph and his protracted reconciliation with his brothers. If you've been wounded and need a patient friend on the fragile path of redemption, I would highly commend *I Forgive You*."

J. Alasdair Groves, Executive Director, CCEF

"In this fallen world, none of us are immune from hurt or hurting others. If we're honest, most of us find forgiveness hard. In this easy-to-read book, Wendy Alsup gives us space to wrestle with the complexity of forgiveness and encouragement to desire it. Our eyes are lifted to the God who is sovereign, gracious, and kind—and that's always a hope-filled place for a struggling Christian to gaze toward."

Helen Thorne, Director of Training and Resources,
Biblical Counselling UK

"There is no better guide than Wendy Alsup to the important but difficult terrain of forgiveness and reconciliation. Drawing with honesty upon her own stories of deep hurt and bringing the Scriptures to life in profound ways, Wendy offers a deeply hopeful vision of God's ability to bring reconciliation in seemingly impossibly broken situations and to give us peace even when our relationships fall short of God's vision for them. A beautiful and rich reflection, shaped by deep biblical wisdom on every page."

Kristen Deede Johnson, Professor of Theology and Christian
Formation, Western Theological Seminary

"This book reveals Wendy Alsup at her best. She has a gift for making Scripture accessible, compelling, and relevant. I've read dozens of books on forgiveness, and *I Forgive You* is my new favorite. It might just be the most compelling, practical, and relevant book on forgiveness you've ever read. "

Dorothy Greco, Author, *Making Marriage Beautiful*

"The healing power of forgiveness is well-attested, but rarely is it presented to us framed so aptly in the Scriptures. Wendy Alsup gives us more than a pat proverb or a hurried how-to. She retells at length an ancient forgiveness story both beautiful and true, interweaving it with her own story of hurt and healing. She invites us to examine our own capacity to fight to forgive by the power of the Spirit of grace that lives within us. As I read, I contemplated with fresh resolve those to whom I could grant forgiveness, and those whose forgiveness I should seek."

Jen Wilkin, Author and Bible Teacher

"Christians rejoice in the wonderful forgiveness we have received in the Lord Jesus Christ, but often find it much harder for forgive others and restore broken relationships when we have been sinned against. This book will bring help, hope, and healing as Wendy Alsup applies biblical principles and practical wisdom from the remarkable story of Joseph to situations in which reconciliation seems impossible. She shares from her own experiences of painful relationship breakdowns and the peace that real repentance, forgiveness, and reconciliation have brought."

John Stevens, National Director, FIEC UK

"Wendy has given the church a great gift. As is her hallmark, she takes us into the Scriptures deeply—this time by immersing us in the story of Joseph. Through keen biblical insights coupled with wisdom forged from decades of following the Lord faithfully—and often at great personal cost—she has written a book that will help make us wiser in the challenging but non-negotiable Christian vocation of loving our enemies. In a day and age when worldly voices and forces are seducing us to seek to destroy our enemies, this is a timely and welcome corrective voice."

Rev. John Haralson, Pastor, Grace Church Seattle

"I have already found myself sharing pieces of transformative wisdom from *I Forgive You.* Joseph's story took on a whole new layer of meaning as Wendy narrated the emotions of his painful betrayal and miraculous forgiveness. Every one of us will experience unexpected and devastating hurt—even from those we love. This book will be a worthy companion that calls wounded souls to the ultimate Healer, who also knew the sting of betrayal and showed us how to release others so we might truly live."

Dorena Williamson, Author, *ColorFull*; Co-Planter, Strong Tower Bible Church, Nashville, TN

"Whether you've been wounded and are seeking to forgive or you're the one who's done the wounding and are wondering how to make amends, Wendy has given you a gift in writing *I Forgive You*. She leads us deeper into the gospel of Jesus, which alone has the power to fix what's broken."

Rev. John Mark Patrick, Pastor, Trinity Presbyterian Church, Orangeburg, SC

"A powerful and much-needed book. Drawing from personal experience and the life of Joseph, Wendy Alsup insightfully shows us the path, process, and price of forgiveness and reconciliation. *I Forgive You* helped me acknowledge my own ambiguous losses and will undoubtedly aid countless others in their journey toward healing and wholeness. Highly recommend!"

Vaneetha Rendall Risner, Author, *Walking Through Fire: A Memoir of Loss and Redemption*

"Wendy Alsup is a theological heavyweight who writes with the real and gentle touch of a friend. Her teaching is biblically rich, spiritually nuanced, deeply wise, and thoroughly relatable. In *I Forgive You*, she applies her powers to one of the hardest questions we face: how to forgive. In these pages, you will fill yourself on God's word in the company of one who knows and cares about your pain. I am so grateful Wendy had the courage to take us on this journey with her—it will be a tremendous resource for us all."

Sharon Hodde Miller, Author, *Free of Me: Why Life Is Better When It's Not about You*

"Wendy understands the feelings of disappointment, grief, and betrayal that linger long after a relationship is severed. She also knows there is hope for healing and restoration—even when it seems impossible. Realistic, vulnerable, and biblically faithful, she is a wise and compassionate guide on the path to forgiveness."

Carolyn Lacey, Author, *Extraordinary Hospitality (For Ordinary People)*

Wendy Alsup

I
FORGIVE
YOU

I Forgive You
© Wendy Alsup, 2022.

Published by The Good Book Company

thegoodbook.com | thegoodbook.co.uk
thegoodbook.com.au | thegoodbook.co.nz | thegoodbook.co.in

Published in association with Don Gates of The Gates Group,
www.the-gates-group.com

Cover design by Faceout Studio, Jeff Miller

ISBN: 9781784986865 | Printed in Turkey

Contents

I am indebted to my pastor, Rev. J.P. Sibley, for faithfully leading our church through the life of Joseph and willingly sharing his sermon notes with me for this book. As much as your teaching on Sunday has impacted my life, J.P., watching you live out these principles daily on the ground in our community has blessed me even more.

Introduction

"I forgive you."

These are simple words, but hard ones. Perhaps they are words you just can't bring yourself to say. Has someone harmed you so deeply you cannot imagine releasing them of their debt to you? Or perhaps these are words you long to hear. Have you harmed a loved one? Does restoring the relationship seem impossible?

Many of us have harmed or been harmed in our marriages. Many of us have harmed or been harmed by our parents or siblings. Many of us have harmed or been harmed through racial insensitivity or downright hostility in our communities. Many of us have harmed or been harmed through church conflict. Or conflict at work. Or a thousand other possible scenarios. Do words of forgiveness—and the reconciliation that may potentially follow—feel far out of your reach?

What would you say if I told you that forgiveness is not out of your reach—that we have a God who loves reconciliation, a Savior who came into the world to reconcile us to himself, and a Spirit who works change and healing among us? That there is hope—even for you?

It's true: there will always be aspects of reconciliation that are out of your control. You can confess your sin to the one you harmed, but you cannot guarantee they will respond with forgiveness. You can forgive the one who has harmed you, but that does not mean they will fully recognize the wrong they have done or repair in the ways that are right. Though you can release them from the place they hold in your mind, a fully reconciled relationship is not always possible.

So what hope is there? When forgiveness and reconciliation seem impossible, how might this book help?

Before we explore the answer to that question, I want to be clear what this book is not. It is not a manual on best practice in situations of continued abuse. If you are currently in an abusive situation, please tell someone who can help you—and keep telling, until someone finally believes you. Don't give up telling the truth of what is happening to you until someone steps up and helps! If you were abused in the past, I encourage you, too, to speak about it with someone you know and trust. I hope you will find the discussion of forgiveness here helpful and hopeful, and not a weight upon you, as you process how to think of the one who has harmed you in the past.

This book is also not a straightforward, step-by-step manual on how to reach reconciliation with another. Though we will go through various aspects of a process of sorts, we will find that this process is messy, with any number of complicating factors that can suddenly turn progress aside. There is no tidy linear path to reconciliation. I like to call it a stew. It helps if, up front, you expect messy complications along the way.

Over the next eight chapters, this book looks at the Bible to find hope for our broken relationships and insight for how to pursue forgiveness and healing—which are both possible, even where full reconciliation is not. Specifically, we will look at the life of Joseph in the book of Genesis. I can think of no better story to give us practical insight for our own complicated, messy situations. In the story of Joseph, his father, and his brothers, God gives a vision of what is possible when all seems lost, when reconciliation seems impossible, and when those we love are far off, seemingly out of our reach. The story of Joseph gives us hope, too, when we are overwhelmed with guilt for the harm we have done against our loved ones.

God loves forgiveness and reconciliation. He loves it so much that he sent Jesus into the world so that he could reconcile us to himself. Jesus endured incredible agony because he loved us and longed to forgive us. And with the help of his Spirit he promises to reconcile us to each other as well.

Broken relationships have been the norm, rather than the exception, ever since Adam and Eve broke the first relationship in the Garden of Eden. But even in their story—as we'll see—God gave us hope that one would come who would defeat Satan and allow sinners to be reconciled once again to God and neighbor. Then, in the very first book of the Bible, God left us the story of Joseph and his brothers to give us insight into his ability to bring reconciliation when it seems impossible and to miraculously use for good circumstances which we can only imagine will end in utter devastation. The story of our Savior gives us hope. The story of Joseph shows us how that hope works out in real life—including *your* real life.

I have experienced many kinds of conflicts and brokenness in my life. Some have seen resolution. Some haven't, yet. Wherever you are in your own journey from brokenness to healing, this book is designed to encourage you to persevere in hope. God is for you. He sees you, and he has a good plan for your life. If you long to move forward but it seems impossible, know that God has not left you as an orphan to navigate this situation by yourself. There is help and hope to persevere.

Before you go on, read Genesis 37 – 50 for yourself—even if you are already familiar with the story of Joseph and his brothers. May your first reading before we dive in whet your appetite for the miracles God can work: to redeem and restore you and others, even when reconciliation seems impossible.

Joseph Wept

THE PAIN OF LOSS

The young man hit the bottom of the dirt pit with a thud. Was his lip bloody? Was his body bruised? I picture him grabbing his head, spitting dirt out of his mouth. Only 17 years old, he couldn't see over the sides of the deep pit into which he had been thrown, but he could hear the voices of his brothers as they ate their dinner by the fire—the very brothers who had just thrown him into the pit. Could he hear their plot to kill him? As he cradled his throbbing head, could he comprehend what was happening to him? Was he in shock? Did he call out to his brothers for help? Was he stunned at how they ignored his cries?

I imagine the teenager hearing the sounds of men and animals moving closer. Hope of being rescued from the pit grew in his heart. Sure enough, his brothers dragged him out—but, instead of apologizing for their brutality, they pushed him into the hostile hands of traders who would only dehumanize him further, treating him as a thing to be used for their own benefit.

Bruised and bound behind a camel, did he struggle to understand this turnaround in his circumstances? Just that morning, he had been the favored son of a man of resources. But now, he was thrust into survival mode, surrounded by men who would meet any weakness with harsh punishment, not compassionate concern. Did he have time to process the betrayal or did survival mode take over?

Genesis 37 – 50 gives us the story of this young man: Joseph, son of Jacob, great-grandson of Abraham. Less than a chapter after we meet him, he has been betrayed by his own brothers and flung into a hostile, unknown world. He will live for decades surrounded by people yet utterly alone.

His brothers' betrayal broke every relationship Joseph had had up to that point in his life, leaving him powerless to do anything except try to survive. He lost the most important things humans need to flourish. He lost love. He lost belonging. He lost trusted relationships. He was alienated from all he had known—from all the relationships that were important to him.

He would live. He would even flourish. But his losses would permanently alter his life and weigh heavily on him for decades.

JOSEPH'S AMBIGUOUS LOSS

It's helpful to have a name for our grief when we experience broken relationships as Joseph did. Therapist and researcher Pauline Boss popularized the phrase "ambiguous loss" (you can read more about it on her website: www.ambiguousloss. com). This is different from a loss such as the death of a loved one—it's less straightforward but still agonizing. It is a type of loss without a culturally recognized way to grieve or reach closure. It can involve *physical absence with psychological presence.* Divorce or estrangement from family, for example—you don't see the person anymore but they are still very present in your mind. Or it can involve *psychological absence with physical presence.* In this case, a loved one is missing emotionally or cognitively, though you still see them regularly in person. Addiction, depression, dementia, and other chronic physical or mental illnesses can result in this type of loss.

Such losses leave us stuck while our family, church, or work relationships go on without us. Other people seem to sail on as we are left treading water in their wake. How do we navigate and grieve these losses when society does not necessarily even recognize them as real loss?

The story of Joseph is a quintessential example of ambiguous loss. Joseph was the first son of Jacob's favorite wife, though he was the eleventh son born to Jacob overall. Jacob favored Joseph over his older sons, setting his family up for jealous rivalries that tore them apart. Though his brothers originally planned to kill Joseph, they instead sold him into slavery. He experienced decades of ambiguous loss as a result—alienated from the father and little brother he loved, only to come face to face unexpectedly decades later with the very brothers that had betrayed him so callously.

For those of us who are living in the middle of unreconciled relationships, even the way Joseph's story is told gives us insight into our own feelings of grief and loss.

MOMENTS OF GRIEF

I imagine Joseph's mind slowing down as he attempted to process what was happening to him. He must have been in shock; his brothers' actions against him were so horrible as to be unimaginable to him. Yet, as time wore on, he woke up to a horror worse than any he'd previously imagined for himself— enslaved in a culture he did not know, at the whim of brutal men. Early on, he found some footing in Potiphar's house, just to lose it all again when Potiphar's wife falsely accused him of rape. What was it like for Joseph to lose footing and security a second time? To be thrown into a jail cell after he had been thrown in a pit? I know from my own experiences that the second round of loss or betrayal is much worse emotionally than the first. We have a phrase for it: Joseph was kicked when he was down.

While in jail, Joseph experienced a third betrayal on top of the first two. He interpreted the dream of Pharaoh's cupbearer, and this man promised to remember Joseph and bring his case to Pharaoh. But he forgot, leaving Joseph in what was likely the foulest place in all of Egypt for another two years. Joseph sat in that dungeon—first betrayed, then falsely accused, and finally forgotten.

Moses wrote most of Joseph's story in matter-of-fact terms. We are left to intuit Joseph's feelings. But there are four scenes that give us insight into the emotions Joseph carried day in and day out as he endured his decades of alienation from the family he loved. Four times, Joseph wept.

By the point when Scripture first tells us of Joseph's weeping, he was on stable footing, second-in-command in Egypt, and a trusted help to Pharaoh. He had a wife and children. He was rich and influential. God had blessed him greatly. Yet these instances of weeping reveal the deep emotions he had long held that were not resolved by his success in Egypt. All the blessings in Egypt could not undo the pain from the losses he had experienced.

These emotional scenes help us understand Joseph as a real person like you and me, struggling to endure his ambiguous loss in the same ways we do. In order for us to find a home in Joseph's story for ourselves, we must put off any notion that he was a superhero, unaffected by the emotional toll of his losses. Joseph struggled as we would in a similar loss. These four glimpses of Joseph's grief serve as a mirror for our own.

"

Joseph was a real person like you and me. His grief serves as a mirror for our own.

"

SCENE 1: THE FIRST MEETING

By Genesis 42, Joseph had finally been elevated from a slave left to rot in jail to second-in-command under Pharaoh, tasked with helping the nation through a long famine. When Joseph's brothers came to buy grain in Egypt, Joseph was the one they went to. He saw them for the first time in over two decades—and though Joseph recognized them, they did not recognize him. Joseph devised a plan to hold one of his brothers hostage to coerce them into bringing his beloved little brother, Benjamin, to him in Egypt. The scene unfolds as, after three days in prison, Joseph told his brothers,

> *If you are honest, let one of you be confined to the guardhouse, while the rest of you go and take grain to relieve the hunger of your households. Bring your youngest brother to me so that your words can be confirmed; then you won't die. (Genesis 42:19-20)*

The brothers then had an agitated discussion among themselves, unaware that Joseph could understand them.

> *"Obviously, we are being punished for what we did to our brother. We saw his deep distress when he pleaded with us, but we would not listen. That is why this trouble has come to us."*

> *But Reuben replied, "Didn't I tell you not to harm the boy? But you wouldn't listen. Now we must account for his blood!"*
> *(v 21-22)*

Can you imagine this moment in Joseph's heart? His last memory of his brothers—the one seared into his psyche for decades—was of their hardened hearts and deaf ears as he cried out for help. His last vision of them was that of the slave-dealers putting money into their hands as wagons pulled Joseph away from the land of his father. What a bitter, foul memory that must have been for Joseph over the last two decades.

For the first time in Joseph's story, Moses records:

He turned away from them and wept. (v 24)

Though Joseph presented himself to his brothers as a stern authority, the reader is made aware of his deep emotional response to hearing their words. "We saw his deep distress when he pleaded with us, but we would not listen ... Now we must account for his blood!" His brothers were finally acknowledging the wrong they had done to him.

Can you imagine what it was like for Joseph to hear this? Perhaps you yourself have wept with relief from hearing such words. Or maybe you still wait with longing to hear the one who harmed you acknowledge what they have done. After years of living in the grief of ambiguous loss, Joseph heard his brothers finally name the harm they had done to him. They finally put words to the reality Joseph had lived. And he wept.

SCENE 2: SEEING BENJAMIN

Genesis 43 sees the brothers return to Egypt a second time, bringing Benjamin, as Joseph had requested. When Joseph saw his little brother Benjamin for the first time in decades, he again broke down weeping.

When he looked up and saw his brother Benjamin, his mother's son, he asked, "Is this your youngest brother that you told me about?" Then he said, "May God be gracious to you, my son." Joseph hurried out because he was overcome with emotion for his brother, and he was about to weep. He went into an inner room and wept there. (Genesis 43:29-30)

Joseph had already come face to face with the ones who caused the losses in his life. He now came face to face with the loss itself. He had lost his relationship with his little brother. The baby of the family, loved and protected by all, had been Joseph's brother in every sense of the word— the only other son of the wife whom their father truly loved. They were full brothers in a dysfunctional family with older half-brothers who resented them because of their father's obvious preference for them. And they had not seen one another for 22 years.

It is hard to imagine the wealth of emotions Joseph faced. Surely he was overjoyed to see his brother. But the baby brother he remembered was now grown up—a young adult. Gone were the chubby cheeks and clumsy attempts to keep up. He stood there tall yet vulnerable before Joseph's authority. There was a gulf between them, a canyon dug deep and wide by the river of more than twenty years of separate experiences.

Maybe you've felt such a gulf between yourself and those with whom you long to be reconciled. It can feel impossible to bridge. Though Joseph knew Benjamin well, did Benjamin even remember Joseph? Face to face, he didn't recognize Joseph, and Joseph wasn't yet ready to reveal himself. The weight of Joseph's ambiguous loss must have been heavy in that moment. Joseph and Benjamin were physically only feet apart. But so much more separated Joseph from this one he loved. The gulf between them was huge. And Joseph wept.

SCENE 3: JOSEPH REVEALS HIMSELF

When Joseph finally revealed himself to his brothers, the dam holding his emotions broke, and he could no longer control his grief or relief.

Joseph could no longer keep his composure in front of all his attendants, so he called out, "Send everyone away from me!" No one was with him when he revealed his identity to his brothers. But he wept so loudly that the Egyptians

heard it, and also Pharaoh's household heard it. Joseph said
to his brothers, "I am Joseph! Is my father still living?" But
they could not answer him because they were terrified in his
presence. (Genesis 45:1-3)

In the first two scenes of weeping, Joseph had managed to
bring his emotions back under control. But now the dam
finally broke. Joseph "ugly cried," and everyone witnessed it.

There was no immediate falling into the arms of his
brothers, though. They responded with terror, not joy, to
the realization that he was still alive. We too may experience
complicated, unexpected, and hurtful responses to our
attempts to bridge the gulf between ourselves and those
we have wronged or who have wronged us. Even when
appropriate first steps are made, it is hard to trust one
from whom we have been long estranged. Reconciliation in
Joseph's family, too, would not be simple.

Joseph sobbed out the question that had been on his heart
for decades: was his beloved father still alive? This question
sets us up for the final scene of Joseph's deep emotions.

SCENE 4: SEEING HIS FATHER

After Jacob learned that Joseph was alive, he headed for Egypt
with all his descendants and all he owned. As he reached the
land of Goshen, on the outskirts of Egypt, Joseph heard that
his father was near and could wait no longer to see him.

Joseph hitched the horses to his chariot and went up to
Goshen to meet his father Israel [another name for Jacob].
Joseph presented himself to him, threw his arms around
him, and wept for a long time.

Then Israel said to Joseph, "I'm ready to die now because I
have seen your face and you are still alive!"

(Genesis 46:29-30)

Finally, the long estrangement of Joseph from his family was over. He held his father, and his father held him—both of them unwilling to let go.

This was a different type of weeping. Joseph was finally reconciled to his long-lost father. They wept for all that had been lost in the decades that had separated them. But they also wept for relief, as the weight that had pressed them both down for so long was finally lifted.

JOSEPH'S LOSS AND YOURS

Joseph first wept at the relief of finally hearing his brothers name their sin against him. He wept the second time when he saw Benjamin and came face to face with the collateral damage of his brothers' betrayal. He wept the third time as he revealed himself to his brothers and again when he hugged the frail bones of his father. The Bible doesn't undercut the reality of the pain in Joseph's story—or your own. How do we forgive when the sins against us harm more than just us? How do we forgive for harm done to our loved ones when we can barely let go of harm done to ourselves? Joseph walks with us in this struggle.

When Joseph finally hugged his father in person, the ambiguous nature of his loss coalesced into something tangible. He faced head-on the reality of the loss, as did his father. They did it together, in each other's arms. Ambiguous loss was over, and the reality of the loss was mourned. But their tears were accompanied by smiles as well, as they hung on to each other for a long while—each finally able to physically touch the one from whom they had been separated for so long.

Perhaps this is what you long for in your own story of loss. Do you long for reconciliation—for acknowledgment of what has been done to you? Do you long to hold the one from whom you've been alienated? Do you long for an easy relationship, for peace where there has been conflict, and for tears of joy where there have only been tears of betrayal?

Or perhaps you don't want any of those things at all. Maybe you would rather never see the person who harmed you again. You are not ready for reconciliation. The emotional toll seems too hard.

As you compare your situation with Joseph's, remember this: each of these scenes of weeping comes at the *end* of Joseph's story. We are watching repentance and restoration begin to take place, but each scene reflects emotions that Joseph had felt for more than two decades. For years, he carried the grief of ambiguous loss with no expectation of anything ever changing. Yet things did change. Joseph's story gives us a vision of how God can supernaturally bring healing even when the way seems impossible.

There were multiple moments in Joseph's story when reconciliation seemed impossible: the gulf too wide and the pain too deep to bridge. Our path to reconciliation is complicated too—and we should acknowledge up front that not all relationships will be reconciled. We feel the grief Joseph felt, but we may not get to feel the relief of reconciliation on this side of eternity. However, that does not mean it is not worth pursuing. Our God does the impossible on a regular basis. He "gives life to the dead and calls things into existence that do not exist" (Romans 4:17). This is God's character, and he is at work in our lives as he was in Joseph's. Open yourself to hope for something better.

Look, I am about to do something new;
even now it is coming. Do you not see it?
Indeed, I will make a way in the wilderness,
rivers in the desert. (Isaiah 43:19)

Our Greatest Need

GOD'S PLAN FOR RECONCILIATION

I sat in the sanctuary of our Seattle megachurch as the charismatic pastor preached on the scene from Nehemiah 13 in which Nehemiah tore out the hair of elders who allowed their daughters to marry idol worshipers. "If I wasn't afraid I'd end up on CNN, I would do that myself to some of my elders right now," the preacher declared, drawing awkward laughter from the crowd in the pews.

My brain slowed down to process what he had just said. Did my pastor just threaten his fellow elders? What had made him so mad at his own co-pastors that he would say such a thing to the entire church? I knew nothing of our elders that would justify such harsh words.

What the pastor had said clashed with what I thought was the spirit of our church leadership. This pastor preached the gospel from the pulpit. The elders I knew personally lived out that gospel practically week by week. We were on mission together to make Christ known in our community. We valued repentance and restoration. If an elder was sinning in some way, wouldn't the leadership go humbly to the elder in question and implore them to repent? The idea of my pastor being so angry with our elders that he wanted to physically harm them simply didn't compute.

The next day, I received an email from the two executive elders of our megachurch. Two of our oldest, most respected elders had been fired. These particular elders were known for their wisdom and maturity in the faith. This letter explicitly said the fired elders were not guilty of a disqualifying moral problem—which only made the situation more confusing.

This church conflict sent me down a path of dissonance that still, to this day, has not been fully resolved. Dissonance is the name we give the sound in an orchestra when two notes conflict with one another. They do not harmonize. Though both exist together, they do not work together. The result is cacophony.

When two elders who believed and preached the good news that Jesus reconciles sinners to God cut off two other elders who believed and preached this same good news, the notes didn't work together in harmony. This action produced a noise in my head that I couldn't resolve.

Our church had long held the core values of "Beauty, Meaning, Truth, and Community." It was there that I first experienced deep community in small groups that ate together, prayed together, got together for holidays, and so forth. The elder that had preached the angry sermon had once offered me respite in his home near the hospital when my husband was in the ICU there. The family of the elder that had been fired had organized meals and companionship for me in the ICU waiting room and in the weeks when my husband was recovering. If community was really a core value in our congregation, how did we end up at this place of conflict between key leaders—the very ones who had been discipling the rest of us in these core values?

Community and fellowship that had been cultivated over years was lost in days. It sent shock waves through the church and through my life and the lives of others. It remains a profound loss.

Do you sit in the ashes of similar long and profound losses? Perhaps your losses, like mine, are among the very Christian brothers and sisters who proclaim the gospel that is supposed to reconcile us to one another. The resulting grief is hard to quantify, but it is real.

A COSTLY LOSS

I now recognize that what I felt through that church conflict was ambiguous loss. It affected me daily, but outwardly it didn't look like loss. There were no culturally recognized ways to navigate or respond. I was physically present with my church family in the first weeks after this new conflict came to light. In an act of tremendous courage, the family of the elder that was fired came to church as well. But though we still worshiped with our church family, something had fundamentally changed between us. We were together, but we were separate in our understanding of the situation. I listened to the same pastor preaching Sunday sermons, but his words now impacted me in a very different way.

In the first weeks of the conflict, I fully expected glorious reconciliation—the kind that would actually strengthen church relationships and our overall testimony in our community. Instead, weeks of unresolved issues stretched into months. This was not God's kingdom coming and his will being done on earth as it was in heaven. How could we live with this dissonance long term?

Then the loss became deeper still. As the months went on, the remaining elders of the church expired every member's church membership. To rejoin the church, I would have to sign a form that said I had no unresolved concerns about how my elders had handled this firing. I knew it would be a lie for me to sign that paper, so I could no longer be a member of this church, in which I was a deaconess and volunteered in discipleship ministry.

I had moved to Seattle from across the country to be a part of this church. It was where I belonged. And now I had to leave. I felt like I had been thrown off a ship which was sailing on without me. Now I was no longer in the presence of this church family whom I had loved and long ministered with. Yet their presence still weighed heavily in my mind. I was physically absent while psychologically present with them. I found myself having conversations with the lead pastor in my bathroom mirror, pleading for repentance and reconciliation. This conflict dominated my head space, but I was powerless to effect any change in the circumstances.

It wasn't just about where I went on a Sunday or about losing the role I had in the church. During the six years I had lived in Seattle, far away from my family on the east coast, I had spent the Thanksgiving holidays with friends from my church community group. These friends had walked with me through serious surgeries, miscarriage, job loss, and the birth of my children. They had become family. But suddenly, the relationship with them was broken. It was a stunning loss. I had loved them, laughed with them, and ministered with them. Our desire to minister in our community had led to intimate spiritual and emotional bonds. How was it possible that we understood the conflict in our church so differently?

The grief that followed infiltrated my life at every level—an undercurrent of demoralization that clouded my mind. I made myself go through the motions, but I could not become excited about anything. I had no enthusiasm. I functioned, but it was a head-down, persevering-against-the-storm kind of functioning.

My family began attending a new church in town, a lovely group of believers who would eventually become dear family. But for many months we sat in the back row each Sunday, last to arrive and first to leave. I couldn't explain at the time, even to myself, why I kept my distance. I needed community, but I felt like I couldn't enter it again. I felt complicated emotions around the losses I'd experienced—ambiguous losses I couldn't even name at that point. Engaging with new people after the loss of so many old friendships did not come easily.

Broken relationships come with a cost. We pay the cost at gatherings of family or friends. Perhaps we are not even invited to such gatherings anymore. We pay the cost when we are alone in our beds at night. We pay the cost on Sunday mornings. The loss of community—wherever it is and whatever the reason for it—hits us at a fundamental level in our psyche.

Why? Why does the loss of community affect us so deeply? When we understand the answer to that question, we are better ready to understand and apply God's remedy for it.

CREATED TO BELONG

It is not good for the man to be alone. (Genesis 2:18)

The first scene between humans in all of Scripture prepares us to understand why it was good and right to hold "Community" as a core value at our megachurch. It helps us understand the depth of the loss Joseph faced as the caravan took him away from his family and former life. And it equips us to understand our own deep grief when such community in our lives is broken.

Stop for a moment and envision the newly formed Garden of Eden. There's a tight green carpet of grass, soft under Adam's feet. The branches of fruit trees touch the ground under the weight of their bounty. Bulls, camels, and tigers meander through the trees. A wolf nudges Adam's hand for a pet. A lamb lies against the side of a lion. It is lush, and it is peaceful. The smell is perfect, the temperature exactly right. The flowers are magnificent. The animals are incredible.

Nevertheless, the Bible says it was not fully good.

Despite the glorious setting, there was something still missing. Despite even the communion that Adam had with God there, there was something still missing. This is profound! Scripture tells us that when everything was perfect in the environment and among the animals, when everything was right between God and Adam, *it was not good that the man was alone.* This statement in Scripture gives great insight into the deepest needs of the human heart. It gives us insight into the hardest burden Joseph faced as a captive among traders who did not care for him as anything but an object to be exploited. And it gives you insight into why you haven't written off your own broken relationships—into why you picked up a book on forgiveness and reconciliation.

Humans need community. We need to love and be loved in order to be fully human. This need for belonging is ingrained deeply in the human psyche because it is foundational to our very creation. Scripture lets us in on a pivotal statement made by the Trinity in Genesis 1:26: "Let us make man in our image, according to our likeness." God the Father, God the Son, and God the Spirit have a perfect relationship. The three Persons of God belong to one another, and they love one another. And the triune God created us in his image: he made us to be like him. That means that love and belonging—just as the members of the Trinity love and belong to one another—are essential for living out our full humanity.

With the creation of man's partner, the woman, in Genesis 2, everything was finally good in the Garden of Eden. Humankind had what they needed to properly image the character of their Creator God in the world. It would take at least two of them, in relationship, loving and belonging to one another. They were now a community.

But we don't have long in Scripture to see perfect relationships between humans as God created them to be. After God created the second human, the woman, as a strong helper in the image of God, Satan entered the scene, tempting her and Adam to sin. All the relationships between humans and God broke in that moment.

Immediately after the fall, God prophesied the long-term harm of broken relationships (Genesis 3:16). There would be strife between these first two humans, the man and the woman, and between all future humans.

Imagine Eve's eyes widening as Adam, for the first time, turned against her to blame her before God: *The woman you gave to be with me—it's her fault.* Did Eve step back, stunned and confused? Did she feel sick in her stomach as she realized that this man, with whom she had enjoyed a perfect relationship, now saw her as the reason for his problems? Did she grow bitter toward him as he grew bitter toward her? And when God's prophecy began to come true, did Adam curse Eve as he plowed ground covered in thorns? Did Eve curse Adam as she screamed in childbirth? Did they blame one another when their son killed his brother?

Broken relationships have characterized humanity ever since that first conflict. Genesis gives us story after story of pain and strife, culminating in the dark story of Joseph's betrayal by his brothers. Incredibly, Joseph's family were God's chosen people, through whom God would eventually bring the Savior. These brothers would become the twelve tribes of Israel. Yet they sinned deeply against one another.

The broken relationships in Jacob's family seemed hopeless. Adam and Eve's alienation from both God and one another seemed hopeless as well—or would have were it not for God's words spoken to Satan in front of them. God promised that one would come, born of a woman, to give a knockout blow to Satan's head (Genesis 3:15). One would come, God said, who would right these wrongs: who would fix this problem of broken community between us and God and between one another, once and for all.

COMMUNITY RESTORED

Fast forward from the early chapters of Genesis, past the story of Joseph, to the book of John. Jesus had come to earth, and he was preparing to die, fulfilling God's promise in Genesis 3:15 of the one who would come, born of woman, to soundly defeat Satan. In John 17, Jesus prayed a final prayer for his disciples before he was crucified to pay for their sins. The content of this prayer is important. It gives us insight into the burdens on Jesus' heart at this crucial moment of discipling his little band of new converts, right before he gave his life to reconcile them and us to God.

Holy Father, protect them by your name that you have given me, so that they may be one as we are one. (John 17:11)

Jesus came not just to reconcile us to God, but to reconcile us to one another as well. He prayed that his disciples would have the kind of community among themselves that the three Persons of God experience in the Trinity. With this prayer, Jesus points us back to that moment in Genesis when the Trinity first spoke among themselves their intention to make us in their image. It should be no surprise since Jesus had just commanded his disciples to love one another as he had loved them (John 13:34-35).

As we become one with Christ, Jesus prayed that we will also become one with one another. Why is reconciliation with others an essential outcome of the gospel? Because it is not good for us to be alone! It is not good for humankind to

"

Broken relationships are not going to be our long-term norm. Love and belonging will be.

"

be alienated from God or from one another. It is not good to be betrayed. It is not good to live abandoned by others. It was not good for Adam to accuse Eve, for Cain to kill Abel, or for Joseph to be sold into the hands of men who would treat him as an animal. The betrayal of Joseph's brothers in Genesis 37 captures the essence of all that was wrong with the world after the fall. It also reflects all that Jesus came to save us from.

It was good that my megachurch listed community as a core value. Community is necessary for every one of us in the body of Christ. Even once we are reconciled to God, it still isn't good for us to be alone. It isn't good for us to have unreconciled conflict that divides us. We were not created for this end. We were created for community. And in Christ we are equipped to make that community work.

Now you are the body of Christ, and individual members of it. (1 Corinthians 12:27)

The good news of Jesus gives us hope. Broken relationships are not going to be our long-term norm. Love and belonging in his church will be. This need was instilled in our DNA when God first created humankind in his image. It was re-instilled in us by the Spirit when God made us part of his family. God is breaking down the walls of hostility that sin brought into the world (Ephesians 2:14). He is reconciling believers to himself and to each other. One day, in the new heaven and new earth, we will be at peace with both God and others, just as we were created to be in Eden. We will live in perfect community. This is good news!

THE PAINFUL PRESENT

In Seattle, as the weeks turned into months and the months into years, I wrestled with the ongoing reality of unreconciled conflict. I knew that unity was supposed to characterize a church body reconciled to God through Jesus, but I felt powerless to move my church family toward that end. Years later, the entire church dissolved under the weight of a different conflict, and the lead pastor left town to start another church, without submitting to the very discipline process he himself had put in place, or ever acknowledging the harm he had done to the families of those two elders he had harshly attacked years before.

Yet, in small but consistent ways, gospel reconciliation began to break through the dark taint of unresolved conflict across our former church family. I got a call some years after the original conflict from an older widow in the dying megachurch. She had been approached by an elder who had sinned against her, but she was uncomfortable meeting with him without a witness. Would I go along?

Yes—but I was as nervous about meeting with this former elder as the widow herself was. When we sat down, though, I was amazed at the conversation. He listened well to the ways she felt harmed by him. He recognized his sin and genuinely sought her forgiveness. While much still remained wrong in the aftermath of that church conflict, that conversation characterized many with other elders and leaders who had facilitated the lead pastor's abusive behavior. Reconciliation had by no means been fully completed, but it was taking place in various forms.

It was a microcosm of how the Christian life of faith goes. Jesus has done all that is necessary to put an end to sin and brokenness, but we still wait to see that reality in all of our lives. We experience God's power at work within us and between us, but there is still so much that is "not yet." Perfect reconciliation is at hand, but there is more to come.

You and I sit in various situations where reconciliation has already taken place. If nothing else, if you are trusting in Christ, you have been reconciled to God through him.

But you and I also sit in situations that have not yet seen the type of reconciliation God alludes to in Genesis 3:15 when he promises someone who will defeat Satan entirely. So, we experience pain and confusion as we wait. We feel the loss of hope as days turn into months and months into years.

Joseph's story is a gift of God's grace to us as we stumble along our own paths. Dark and disturbing though the story is at the start, and convoluted though it gets in the middle, it ends with profound lessons on the character of God that can sustain us through broken relationships. God can knit back together what we could never repair on our own. He reconciled Joseph's family, just as he reconciles us to himself and one another. His grace won the day in the life of Joseph, and that same grace can win the day in our own lives too.

Wherever you are right now—sitting with loss or loneliness, raw pain or weary resignation—believe that one has come who has given a knockout blow to Satan's attempts to alienate us from God and from our brothers and sisters in Christ.

Our relationships, though presently broken, have a different long-term destination, and we have tools through Christ to bring reconciliation—tools that Satan cannot overcome. In Christ, we can and will be one with each other, unified in love and faith, even if we currently live in the pain and loss of broken relationships. As we walk through Joseph's story, believe that this is where we are going together in Christ, and hope.

This hope will not disappoint us, because God's love has been poured out in our hearts through the Holy Spirit who was given to us. (Romans 5:5)

In the Middle

LIVING WHILE WAITING

It is tempting at this point to start marching through the process of reconciliation that plays out between Joseph and his brothers. I want desperately to get to the happy ending. But that would mean skipping past the 20 years of ambiguous loss that Joseph endured to get to the glorious resolution found in the very last chapters of Genesis. It would be a mistake to go to the end of Joseph's story without thinking more about his time suspended in the middle. Most likely, more of us are sitting in the years of waiting for reconciliation than actually beginning the process. More are sitting metaphorically in the dungeon waiting for the cupbearer to remember them than sitting in power listening to their brothers acknowledge their sin against them. So, I want to reckon honestly with the struggles of long seasons of waiting. You and I need hope here. Joseph offers us such hope.

Joseph was 17 years old when he was sold into slavery and 28 when he interpreted the cupbearer's dream while in the dungeon. Despite the great help Joseph had been to him, it would be another two years before the cupbearer remembered to mention Joseph to Pharaoh. When he did, Joseph had an opportunity to earn Pharaoh's trust by interpreting his dreams. He was quickly made second-in-command over the whole of Egypt. Instead of the dungeon master controlling Joseph's fate, Joseph now controlled his. Instead of sleeping in the stinking pit, Joseph now directed others from Pharaoh's palace. While Potiphar had sent Joseph to jail, Joseph now had the power to send him. It was a stunning turn of events.

But even this turn for good did not repair the broken things in Joseph's life. He still had no idea if his father was alive or dead. He still had not seen his beloved little brother for over a decade. These losses lay heavy on his heart. At this point in his story, Joseph sat exactly where many of us do—in the middle of the fallout of unreconciled betrayal with no end in sight.

How do we know Joseph's losses still weighed on his heart? Apart from the moments of weeping we examined in chapter 1, we get insight into his struggle in Genesis 41. Pharaoh gave Joseph an Egyptian wife who bore him two sons. Joseph gave both sons Hebrew, not Egyptian, names. Though he had finally found stable footing in Egypt, he still ultimately identified with his homeland and family of origin. This land in which he had fathered his children was not his ultimate home. Joseph chose Hebrew names for his sons with a view both of his losses and of his current status in the land of his captivity. Each name has something to teach us about Joseph's years of loss and waiting. They have something to teach us about ours as well.

HEBREW NAMES FOR HEBREW SONS

Joseph named the firstborn Manasseh and said, "God has made me forget all my hardship and my whole family."
(Genesis 41:51)

The name "Manasseh," which sounds like the Hebrew word for "forget," is truly a paradox. Joseph lived in Egypt, ruled in Egypt, and married an Egyptian woman, but he gave his firstborn son a Hebrew name. Despite naming his son Forget, he clearly hadn't forgotten his heritage completely. Joseph had not passively forgotten his family and his history, as the cupbearer did when he forgot about Joseph. Instead, Joseph seems to be using the word forget in a more active way. He was choosing to forget. He was "forgetting what is behind and reaching forward to what is ahead," as the apostle Paul says in Philippians 3:13.

This kind of forgetting is as much about embracing what lies ahead as it is about leaving behind the past. In Paul's case, it was about pursuing "the prize promised by God's heavenly call in Christ Jesus" (v 14). In Joseph's case, it was about the good future he had in the land of Egypt.

Pharaoh had given Joseph noble work. He tasked Joseph with preparing the land and people to survive a devastating famine that would last for years. Joseph's leadership would be responsible for saving millions of lives. He was also engaged in the noble work of raising the next generation of Israelites. He would raise his sons to know the Lord that he had met in his youth. As he named his firstborn son, Joseph actively forgot the betrayals of the past to focus on the good work ahead of him of saving millions of people from starvation.

Joseph wasn't pretending that the sins against him never happened. The vignettes of Joseph's weeping that we saw in chapter 1 prove that. This was no glib "forgiving and forgetting." The name Manasseh simply signified that the good work God had given Joseph to do in Egypt, not the betrayals of his past, would now define his days.

Joseph named his second son "Ephraim," which sounds like the Hebrew word for "fruitful." He gives his reason for choosing this name in Genesis 41:52:

God has made me fruitful in the land of my affliction.

I was first struck by the name Ephraim as I read through the life of Joseph in April 2009. It was a year after the elders had expired everyone's membership. I had lost the ministry to which I thought God had called me: discipling women in theology at this megachurch that had greatly impacted my city. I could not yet say with the apostle Paul that I was pressing forward, forgetting what was behind. My family had not yet confidently embraced our new church. In every season of my life so far, church ministry had been a constant, but now I felt adrift. I was far from physical family, alienated from the spiritual family I had built in its place, and without tangible work to give myself to. Our pastor's anger and unrepentant sin against church members altered the trajectory of the lives of many other families as well. We had been cast off the ship in the middle of the ocean. We were still treading water, trying to find footing again.

As my friends still in the megachurch sailed on without me, I longed for the boat to return and make things right. I needed help to get back on sure footing, especially when it came to my purpose in God's kingdom. When I read Joseph's reason behind his son's name, it struck me deeply. *God has made me fruitful in the land of my affliction.* This one sentence turned my understanding of the losses around this church conflict on its head.

My first reaction to this name was negative. I didn't want to be fruitful in the land of my affliction. I wanted this affliction to end. Forgetting the past and going on fruitfully in the future felt like acquiescing to another's sin. Would I be accommodating someone's sin against me if I tried to make the best of it?

But as the phrase settled in my mind, I began to understand it differently. Perhaps there was another way to look at this time of waiting for God to resolve this conflict. Was it possible to be fruitful in the very places that threatened to suck the life out of me? Could it be that fruitfulness in this season didn't signify giving in to what had happened but receiving a blessing from God in spite of it?

Eight years later, the name Ephraim would strike me again after a divorce I did not want. As a single mom trying to raise two middle-school boys, I had just started to get my feet back under me when I was diagnosed with breast cancer. Each new trial felt like a wave in the ocean pushing me back underwater, just as I'd managed to get to the surface gasping for breath.

Once again, the name Ephraim gave me a different perspective. Perhaps the image of being in an ocean overcome by waves was the wrong one. Joseph was fruitful in the land, not the ocean, of his affliction. Though it was hard to find footing in these new situations in my life, maybe there was footing to be had if I would put my feet down to feel for it. Instead of treading water, waiting on the boat to return and make things right, maybe I could find land and plant seeds.

I wasn't sure I wanted to stand up in this new and different land I found myself in. I didn't want to be divorced. I didn't want to have cancer. I couldn't envision anything good coming out of this new territory. It felt like giving in to all that was wrong in my life, to try to find footing on this new rocky ground. No, I was going to tread water, hanging on until the ship came back and made things right. After all, Joseph would have been justified in folding his arms in the dungeon and stubbornly declaring, "You have no right to do this to me!"

But you can't tread water forever. And some boats are not going to return anytime soon to pluck you out of the waves. Visions of a vast ocean with no returning boat in sight left me with no agency, flailing in the waves while waiting on others to do the right thing. It did my head and heart good to stop seeing myself in an ocean overcome by loss, and instead envision myself on dry, though unfamiliar, terrain. I could stand up, even if my legs were shaky. I could explore, even if I didn't know where I was going. I could plant, even if I didn't know exactly what would sprout up.

Whether the land in which you find yourself is familiar or foreign—the territory you planned for yourself or not—the names Joseph gave his sons can give you direction. The name Manasseh reminds us which direction we are heading in. The name Ephraim gives us hope for fruitfulness there.

PLANTING SEEDS

Once we put our feet down on the rocky ground of our affliction, we can think about what it means to be fruitful there. Look around the land you find yourself in. In your home, your workplace, your neighborhood, or your church, what ground needs cultivation? What package of seeds has God left at your feet that you can plant?

For Joseph, fruitfulness meant physical flourishing. He had lost all of his family and possessions through his brothers' betrayal, but he now had a wife, children, power, and resources. God had providentially watched over and blessed his life. Joseph was fruitful personally in every physical sense. More importantly, his leadership resulted in fruitfulness nationally: a stored-up harvest that blessed people far and wide during a famine that could have stolen everything.

After my divorce, I could no longer afford to live in Seattle on my income as an author and part-time community-college instructor. I had to leave my home and the only city my kids had known to move to the safety net of family on the east coast. I had invested in ministry at two churches and discipled many women in Seattle. I had also invested in my kids' school, serving in the PTA and actively volunteering in a school with great needs and opportunities. Now I was leaving it all. All of my investments in my community over the last decade seemed for nothing.

In particular, our community elementary school in Seattle had students speaking 63 different native languages at home. Our neighborhood was a true melting pot. But our PTA was made up entirely of white moms. The reasons were varied. As we began to ask questions, we found that some of our parents lacked adequate transportation and many had inflexible job schedules. We also realized that the PTA culture we had unintentionally created was simply uninviting. I helped lead a cohort of PTA moms fumbling through the process of better representing all of our students. We went to training, and we actively worked to recruit folks from other backgrounds and ethnicities to join our board in positions of leadership. We were just starting to see real change when I found myself having to move away, back to a functionally segregated area of the South.

One of the hardest aspects of this move to the South for me was around the issue of race. Long after the Civil Rights Movement, my hometown remained mostly segregated. At the integration of the local school district, white families of resource and influence had formed an association of private schools that explicitly did not allow black students to attend—until the government forced them to integrate in the mid-1980s by threatening to take away their tax-exempt status. Churches remained mostly segregated. The gap between the haves and the have-nots in my community, after centuries of systemic injustice, was staggering. It overwhelmed me to consider the struggles there in light of the work we had begun in our PTA in Seattle.

But an unexpected thing happened after I moved home. Unbeknown to me before the move, my denomination was planting a new church in my old community: one with an eye toward ministry across ethnic, cultural, and economic divides. They already had a diverse leadership team and a diverse core group of believers that genuinely loved and served one another and the larger community. To my astonishment, instead of losing ministry opportunities in this move, I found the one God had been preparing me for all along. It wouldn't

"

We are most fruitful
when God transforms
us internally. This is
miraculous to me.

"

be flamboyant megachurch ministry. It would be quiet work on the ground in an obscure county in South Carolina. But since we moved, I have seen good seeds planted and real fruit being harvested. I have experienced deep and unexpected joy as a part of that ministry—a ministry built by God, to which I was funneled down not by my own foresight or wisdom but through hard circumstances out of my control.

There was land to stand on where before I could only see ocean. There were seeds to plant and fruit to harvest where before I could only see storms and waves.

FRUIT THAT LASTS

For some, the fruitfulness we experience despite our afflictions is physical. Joseph experienced the physical blessings of power, influence, and a new family. Because the cost of living is much lower in the South, I personally am on a better footing financially than I was in Seattle. But physical fruit is not the primary fruit we are offered in Scripture. It pales in comparison to spiritual fruit. While a good physical harvest was regularly a sign of God's blessing on his children in the Old Testament, it is spiritual fruit that dominates the discussion of fruit in the New Testament church. We are most fruitful in the land of our affliction when God transforms us internally.

> *The fruit of the Spirit is love, joy, peace, patience, kindness, goodness, faithfulness, gentleness, and self-control.*
> *(Galatians 5:22-23)*

It is this spiritual fruit that is the most miraculous to me. During my divorce and after my cancer diagnosis, I could not imagine ever being happy again. Joy and peace were spiritual fruits that seemed particularly out of reach. Where was the goodness in the wake of divorce? Where was the joy in breast cancer? I look back now and marvel that there *has* been goodness and joy. I have experienced peace, God has equipped me with faithfulness, and my love for God and my neighbor has grown, not been weakened, through the years of the afflictions associated with both of these trials in my life. This is a miracle of God's grace.

It was the same for Joseph. It's unclear exactly how God led Joseph—but it is clear that it was God who was funneling him down to the place where he had planned for him to flourish: a place God in which would eventually cause his entire extended family to settle and prosper. It was by God's grace that Joseph gained—and gave—the blessings he did. "The LORD was with Joseph," Genesis 39:2 tells us.

The Lord is with you and me, too. Jesus teaches clearly in John 14 – 15 how God is with us now, after Jesus' return to heaven.

I will ask the Father, and he will give you another
Counselor to be with you forever. He is the Spirit of truth.
The world is unable to receive him because it doesn't see
him or know him. But you do know him, because he
remains with you and will be in you. I will not leave you as
orphans. (John 14:16-18)

Jesus sent his Spirit to live inside his disciples. That Spirit would counsel them in the teachings of Christ, reminding them of all he had taught them in person. The Spirit would equip and empower them to go forward into the world and do what they could never do by themselves. The result, Jesus told them, would be fruit that lasts.

I appointed you to go and produce fruit and that your fruit
should remain, so that whatever you ask the Father in my
name, he will give you. (John 15:16)

Particularly after my divorce, I longed for fruit that wouldn't be taken away. I longed to invest in work that someone else couldn't sabotage. How could I invest myself in a new ministry in a new city at a new church after the losses of my previous ministry, community, friends, and home? Jesus gave me the answer to that in the same instructions he gave his disciples.

> *Remain in me, and I in you. Just as a branch is unable to produce fruit by itself unless it remains on the vine, neither can you unless you remain in me. (John 15:4)*

When we sit in the ash heap of our own losses, waiting on someone to recognize their sin against us, Jesus may seem far away. But he promised that he would not leave us as orphans. He is with us even now.

STEPPING FORWARD

How do we abide or remain in Jesus when we can't see or hear him audibly? Practically speaking, I found great help in reading about Jesus in the Gospel of Luke, and, in the book of Acts, about how the Spirit first indwelled believers and continued the work Christ had begun on earth. The Spirit of Christ worked through God's word to give me a vision for flourishing in the land of my affliction—something Jesus did every day he walked the earth.

Are you living in a hard season of affliction, caught in a physical or emotional prison of some type as you wait for God to release you? The book of Hebrews may also be a help to you. Written to Jewish Christians dispersed through intense persecution, Hebrews reminds readers of all we have in Christ despite our current trials. The author encourages Hebrew believers with the truth that Jesus equips us to persevere in places and circumstances that are hard and oppressive. Because of our great high priest, Jesus, we can hold fast to our confession. He was tempted just like us, and he understands our weaknesses. We can approach him boldly to find grace in our time of need (Hebrews 4:14-16). The Spirit of God works through the word of God to grow in us the fruits only he can grow. He helps us to stop treading water and step forward, even in the land of affliction.

As we wait on reconciliation, the names Joseph gave his sons encourage and equip us. Forget what is behind and position yourself toward the work that is ahead. Believe that, in Christ, you can bear eternal fruit that lasts. Prayerfully cultivate the patches of ground God has given you. Look for the little bags of seeds God has left at your feet to plant.

God was with Joseph in the land of his affliction, he was with the early church in theirs, and he is with you and me in the same way now. Unreconciled conflict cannot rob us of the supernatural fruit—fruit that lasts—that Jesus harvests in our lives. In the waiting for things to be made right, dwell in the land you have been given, even if it is not the one you want, and cultivate faithfulness there (Psalm 37:3). Though the field you have been given is not the one you planned, the seeds left to sow may yet yield fruit that will surprise and bless you.

Those who sow in tears
will reap with shouts of joy.
Though one goes along weeping,
carrying the bag of seed,
he will surely come back with shouts of joy,
carrying his sheaves. (Psalm 126:5-6)

The Reckoning

RECOGNIZING THE WRONG

"Can't we all just get along?"

In the spring of 1992, Rodney King spoke those famous words. Los Angeles police officers had been caught on camera beating and kicking King as he lay on the ground after a high-speed chase. The officers were charged for using excessive violence, but all were acquitted. Violent rioting broke out in the city. As protests raged on, King begged on television for peace in the community.

Rodney King longed for peace and was weary of conflict. But the rioting in Los Angeles lasted for six long days, resulting in 63 deaths, 2,383 injuries, more than 7,000 fires, and nearly $1 billion in financial losses. Reconciliation and peace in Los Angeles would not come easily. In the face of the acquittal of the officers who beat King, folks wouldn't just all get along.

Do you identify with King's words? Do you miss things as they were before conflict tore your relationships apart? Do you despair of ever recovering what has been lost? Do you wish folks could simply get along?

South African Anglican bishop Desmond Tutu, who headed South Africa's Truth and Reconciliation Committee at the end of apartheid, teaches in *The Book of Forgiving* that forgiving and being reconciled to our enemies or our loved ones is not about pretending that things are not as they are. It is not telling your opponent that what they did was ok or turning a blind eye to the harm they have done. Instead, true reconciliation begins by facing head on the horror of the acts of conflict.

> *True forgiveness ... is a deep and thorough look at the reality of a situation. It is an honest accounting of both actions and consequences. (The Book of Forgiving, p 58)*

We won't all get along until we have been honest about what brought us to the place of conflict to begin with. Exposing the truth, the awfulness of abuse and harm, is risky. It could make things worse. But only an honest confrontation with reality can bring real healing. "Healing and reconciliation demand an honest reckoning," says Tutu (p 24). There is no other way to true reconciliation. There is no other way to truly get along in community together. We must confess the wrong we have done. Sin must be named.

> *The one who conceals his sins*
> *will not prosper,*
> *but whoever confesses and renounces them*
> *will find mercy. (Proverbs 28:13)*

RECONCILIATION BEGINS

While Joseph was fruitful in the land of his affliction, he was still afflicted. No one had yet acknowledged the sins done against him. He had not yet seen his beloved father and baby brother. He had not yet experienced the reconciliation and healing that Bishop Tutu describes.

In Genesis 42, that opportunity finally came. 22 years after his brothers had sold him into slavery, Joseph came face to face with them in Egypt. But he did not immediately embrace them. He did not implore them to just get along. Reconciliation in Joseph's life turned out to be a convoluted process. It was not superficial. The path he and his brothers followed models for us key principles about confession, repentance, forgiveness, and reconciliation which are taught throughout Scripture.

In Genesis 42 – 45, Joseph's brothers *recognize their offense against Joseph, repent of their wrongdoing, receive forgiveness, and begin to repair the damage they have done.* (I am indebted to my pastor, Rev. J.P. Sibley, for his sermon series in 2020 which outlined these steps of the story.) Though I've summed the process up in a tidy sentence, their story is not tidy at all. Our stories of repentance and reconciliation are rarely tidy either. This is what makes Joseph's story especially helpful to us, whether we have been the cause of the broken relationship or the one harmed by another's sin. The end result in Joseph's family was a restored, albeit different, relationship between the brothers—one that blessed the entire family and led to their flourishing overall.

Before any restoration could take place, the brothers first had to recognize the weight of their sin against Joseph. There is no way around this first step, this gateway, to the path of true reconciliation for any of us. That's true if we are the one who sinned. It's also true, as we'll see, for the one who has been sinned against. Recognition of sin—both of what we have done and of what has been done against us—is vital.

THE RECKONING

After famine hit the land of Canaan, Joseph's father, Jacob, heard that there was grain in Egypt. He sent ten of his sons to buy grain as time was running out to feed his own family.

He did not send his youngest son, Benjamin, though; he feared that something might happen to him. The loss of Joseph still weighed heavily on Jacob's heart, two decades later.

> *When the brothers arrived in Egypt to buy grain, Joseph recognized them, though they did not know him. His brothers came and bowed down before him with their faces to the ground. When Joseph saw his brothers, he recognized them, but he treated them like strangers and spoke harshly to them.*
>
> *"Where do you come from?" he asked.*
>
> *"From the land of Canaan to buy food," they replied.*
>
> *(Genesis 42:6-7)*

As Joseph's brothers bowed before him, Joseph remembered the dreams he had had in his youth, in which his brothers, represented by sheaves of wheat and then stars, bowed down to him. This was the moment that God's prophecy to him was fulfilled! Joseph then set up a test for them. They claimed that they were all brothers—but he accused them of being spies.

> *Send one from among you to get your brother. The rest of you will be imprisoned so that your words can be tested to see if they are true. If they are not, then as surely as Pharaoh lives, you are spies! (v 16)*

If they weren't spies as they claimed, then they should be able to produce the evidence of their story in the form of their little brother.

Of course, Joseph knew their story was true. So, what was his motive for this test? Presumably, he wanted to be restored to his father and his little brother. The loss of those relationships was what had hurt him the most. But what were his intentions toward his older brothers—did he want to be reconciled with them too?

Joseph put his brothers in custody for three days. Perhaps he simply needed more time to think how to respond to the unexpected surprise of seeing them after so many years. His immediate goal was to have them bring his brother and father to him, but he needed a plan to entice them to do that without revealing himself to them. If he told them he was Joseph and sent them to get their father and brother, they might just run in fear of retribution the moment he let them go. Keeping one or most of the brothers in custody in Egypt would ensure their return.

Whatever Joseph's motivation for detaining his brothers, it had a profound consequence in their hearts. Joseph accused his brothers, imprisoned them, and held them in Egypt. These were the very things that had been done to Joseph two decades before. Without saying it explicitly, Joseph was sending his brothers to think about what they had done. Just as time to reflect helps our children see their sin, so those days in jail brought a harsh light to the brothers' sins against Joseph.

THE HARSH LIGHT OF TROUBLE

The brothers did not like being slowed down and accused. They were initially defensive. "We are honest," they claimed (v 11). But their claim of moral goodness was a smoke screen.

I am a good person.
I am not racist.
I didn't mean to offend you.
I've never done anything like this before.

Too often, we see only our best intentions. Pride keeps us from recognizing the ways in which we have offended others, and this stops reconciliation cold. But a season of trouble can open our eyes to the harm we have done against others. When the lens of pride obscures our vision of our own actions, trouble humbles us, grinding down that lens so that we can see our own sinful actions and responses with moral clarity.

After Joseph's brothers had spent three days detained, Joseph repeated his instruction to bring their youngest brother to him so he could verify their story. The brothers talked between themselves in Hebrew, not knowing that Joseph could understand them.

> *They said to each other, "Obviously, we are being punished for what we did to our brother. We saw his deep distress when he pleaded with us, but we would not listen. That is why this trouble has come to us."*
>
> *But Reuben replied, "Didn't I tell you not to harm the boy? But you wouldn't listen. Now we must account for his blood!" (Genesis 42:21-23)*

Finally, the brothers' years of deception and denial came to an end. Their three days in the holding cell forced them to face their sin against Joseph as they got a taste of what they had put their own brother through. *We deserve this,* they said. *We deeply harmed our brother.*

Joseph understood every word.

TAKING STOCK

Let's be clear: trouble comes on the righteous too sometimes. God gave us the story of Job to make that obvious. Suffering is not always a sign of sin—but it can be. So when trouble comes upon us, it's worth paying attention and taking stock. That's what the brothers were doing in Genesis 42.

They knew that God had brought this trouble on them, but they did not fully understand why. As they faced head on the way they had harmed Joseph, they felt only despair. "Now we must account for his blood!" they cried. Their guilt overtook them. They certainly deserved such a reckoning, and it was good that they recognized the weight of their sin against Joseph. But they viewed God as vindictive, expecting payback from him for what they had done. They expected merciless revenge.

Was God paying Joseph's brothers back? As the story plays out, we will see that there was no eye for an eye or tooth for a tooth here.

God was not writing a Hollywood-style revenge movie, designing a storyline for maximum payback. He did not send this trouble into the brothers' lives to get retribution but to provoke repentance. He designed this hard providence to change the brothers' hearts and make a new path for their family as a whole. Change could only start when the brothers finally named their sin for the atrocity it was. They needed to account for what they had done. But the sum on the books after this accounting would be paid with grace, not retribution.

To account means to take stock in an accurate way: to look at the receipts, one might say. God designed circumstances that forced Joseph's brothers to read their receipts. Their days in custody forced them to consider what it meant to sell someone into slavery, to deny them their freedom. They were forced to survey accurately what they had done to their brother, as they temporarily lost their own freedom and were kept from their own families.

Before real reconciliation can take place, such an accurate accounting is a necessary first step.

I lied to you.
I harmed you.
I committed adultery in my heart.
I stole from you.
I was envious of your success.
I despised you.
I treated you as less than human.

Many reading this have been wronged by another. Some reading this recognize themselves as the one who committed the wrong. Few of us are exclusively in only one of those categories. There is value in self-examination for us all.

If God has designed harsh circumstances in your life to cause you to face your sin, receive it as the severe mercy it is. Confess your sin. Face it head on. It is God's kindness, not his vengeance, that calls you to name your sin accurately. "Confess your sins ... so that you may be healed," James tells us (James 5:16). This is good and right. This is necessary for real reconciliation.

For the first time, Joseph heard his brothers own the wrong they had done to him. They named it, validating the reasons that Joseph had to bring vengeance on them if he wanted to. He turned away and wept.

A STARK, RUGGED CROSS

If you are facing the fallout of your sin against another as Joseph's brothers were, the Christian gospel is good news. Yet this good news starts with a hard reckoning. It starts with an accounting of our sin against God and others. Everyone who comes to Christ faces their own sin head on when they look at Jesus' cross. The story of Good Friday is the stark reminder of all that our sin cost Jesus.

Our Savior despaired in the garden, knowing what faced him. He felt physical agony on the cross from the nails in his hands and the open wounds on his back. He cried in anguish, "My God, my God, why have you abandoned me?" (Matthew 27:46). He endured physical and spiritual agony in place of us, for our sin.

I am not contriving a segue from Joseph's story to the cross of Jesus in an attempt to make this a "gospel-centered" book. The cross isn't a sideline motif in Scripture. It is the culmination of thousands of stories like Joseph's. Genesis 37 – 50 tells us one story of sin against God and others. The cross tells us ten thousand. We, like Joseph's brothers, have chosen our own interests to the harm of others. We have chosen ourselves over God. The stark, rugged cross reflects to us what the days in custody showed Joseph's brothers. We are the cause of Jesus' anguish just as Joseph's brothers were the cause of their brother's and father's. The cross is the reckoning for us all.

My worst experience of physical pain came when I had my mastectomy. I opted to have immediate reconstruction of my breast, oblivious to how physically challenging that additional surgery would be. After the surgery, I lay in the ICU for three days in agony, despite the morphine pump that I could push every ten minutes for an additional injection. As I lay awake that first night, crying in misery, I felt the Spirit with me, reminding me that I wasn't alone. Jesus had endured such pain for me—but without opiates to reduce the agony. I had gone through my surgery for my own benefit and healing, but Jesus did not go through his agony on the cross for his own benefit. He did it to pay for my sins, to reconcile me to God. Joseph's brothers felt in that jail cell just a fraction of the pain they had caused Joseph. Similarly, I felt the weight of what the cross cost Jesus as I endured a fraction of such pain myself.

Our offense against God was so severe that only the death of his own beloved Son would bring reconciliation. Many want to call themselves Christians without facing up to their own sin, but the gospel means nothing if we do not recognize our offense against the holy God, which separated us from him in the first place. When we look at the cross, we have a choice between defensiveness, self-condemnation, or humility. Humbly facing the weight of our sin is the response that sets us down the path to true reconciliation with God and others.

That night in the hospital room, my understanding of Christ's agony on the cross grew hour by hour as I endured my own. I did not feel condemnation from God; there is no condemnation for those of us who are in Christ Jesus (Romans 8:1). Instead, I felt humbled by Jesus' sacrifice for me. He endured for my sake what I could not endure for myself. I felt his love and his sacrifice, and I was comforted.

God's kindness leads us to be honest about our sin. He gives us grace as we recognize the seriousness of our offenses against God and others. But few people want to be truthful about their sin. In our culture we love to shift blame, mitigating our reasons for hurting others. Our culture also loves to "cancel" those whose sin is exposed—leading us to spend much of our lives covering over our sins out of shame and fear.

But to those willing to humbly face their sins, God gives grace.

FACING JACOB

Though the process of reconciliation between Joseph and his brothers had begun, it would not come easily. Joseph bound Simeon in front of the rest of the brothers to ensure that they would bring Benjamin back as requested. Then he gave orders to fill the brothers' bags with grain and provisions for their journey home. On top of that, he returned all of their money, which they had given him for food. He was determined to provide for his family without taking their money.

The brothers, however, did not understand Joseph's gift this way. When they found their money returned to them in their sacks, they trembled with fear. "What has God done to us?" they asked one another (Genesis 42:28).

Would the Egyptians think they had stolen their money back? Would they be arrested again if they returned as promised with Benjamin? They knew what they deserved from God, and it was not to have their money returned to them along with food and supplies for their journey.

When they returned to their father, the brothers told him everything that had happened and showed him the money returned to them. They had owned up to their sin against Joseph with one another. Now they had to face how much they had harmed their father by that same betrayal. Jacob was deeply distressed.

It's me that you make childless. Joseph is gone, and Simeon is gone. Now you want to take Benjamin. Everything happens to me! (Genesis 42:36)

Reuben responded by offering a sacrificial commitment to his father. "You can kill my two sons if I don't bring him back to you," he told him (v 37). This was a rash, harsh statement that Jacob would never accept—but it showed that Reuben was thinking about the retribution he deserved for robbing Jacob of his son.

Jacob had to choose between letting Benjamin go to Egypt and abandoning Simeon there. Faced with this agonizing decision, Jacob resisted Reuben's words. He would not let the brothers go back.

As Desmond Tutu said, true reconciliation exposes the awfulness of the abuse and the true nature of the harm done. This is where we find ourselves in the story of Joseph's family. At this point, the brothers had faced their sin against their brother and father. It was ugly. The loss of Joseph had broken Jacob's heart. Now Simeon seemed lost as well. Jacob lamented that the loss of a third child would kill him. The brothers faced their father's agony, knowing that they were responsible for it. There was no path forward without this reckoning of the harm they had done.

GRACE FOR THE ONE HARMED

Many of us sit waiting for such a reckoning in our own story—waiting for the one who has harmed us to recognize the harm they have done. We wait for God to orchestrate circumstances that draw our opponent to repentance after our own attempts have fallen short. As we read of Joseph's brothers finally naming their sin, we long to hear someone name their sin against us. We ache for the validation of the pain we have endured. But we are not left to wrestle with that pain alone.

> LORD, *you have heard the desire of the humble;*
> *you will strengthen their hearts.*
> *You will listen carefully,*
> *doing justice for the fatherless and the oppressed*
> *so that mere humans from the earth may terrify*
> *them no more. (Psalm 10:17-18)*

If you have been harmed, your opponent may never accurately confess how they harmed you. But sometimes, a third party can help you by naming the sins done to you when the one who harmed you can't or won't.

The week that Larry Nassar was sentenced for molesting vulnerable young gymnasts, I watched the video of his accusers in the courtroom. I was sobered by his conviction, with all the life lessons that his fall from celebrated Olympic doctor to sex offender symbolized. But I was gutted by the victim impact statements of the young girls who had accused him. For years, colleagues at USA Gymnastics and Michigan State University had minimized and undermined the young women who tried to bring attention to what Nassar was doing, allowing many more to be molested in their wake. These women had been left to pick up the pieces of their lives as Nassar continued to flourish professionally. His conviction meant that someone finally believed them. A court was finally saying, "Yes, he abused you." If Nassar wouldn't name the harm he had done, a judge would pronounce his guilt and sentence nonetheless.

If you have ever had someone accurately name their sin against you, you know the power in such a moment. But not everyone will see their sin against you clearly. This is

"

God listens carefully, and
he is just. He leans toward
us and works on our behalf.

"

particularly true when issues of mental illness are involved; the person may simply be unable to recognize what they have done.

I wracked my brain for months trying to figure out what mistakes I had made to bring about the circumstances that led to my divorce. I experienced a powerful moment when a counselor I was seeing clearly named some of the sins done against me. I wasn't crazy. I hadn't brought this all on myself. Some healing began to take place in my own heart through the accurate naming of the harm done to me—even if I was not yet able to be reconciled with the one who had done it.

Just as the judge at Larry Nassar's sentencing sat listening to his accusers, accurately acknowledging the sins against them and how he had harmed them, so God sits with all of us. He listens carefully, and he is just. He leans toward the fatherless and oppressed with compassion and care. He promises that total justice will one day be ours. What a great comfort that, while we wait on others to acknowledge their sins against us, the just God of the universe knows, cares, and works on our behalf.

Whether the issue is large-scale, like racial reconciliation in the United States, or more personal, like a broken relationship between friends or family members, we can get frustrated with a process that is long and involved. We want to skip the painful parts and move right to holding hands at the end. We want to enjoy our place at Pentecost without accounting for our part in Gethsemane. Accurately accounting for the harm done to ourselves or others is a hard but necessary step toward true reconciliation.

Joseph's story gives us a real-life picture of men forced to stop and reckon with their history. We too must search our hearts. We must remember, even when it is deeply painful to do so. We must put ourselves in our opponent's shoes. We must be honest, and we must be humble. Reconciliation will not be achieved without an accurate accounting of our offense against God and those we have harmed.

But the good news—the best news—is that the cross of Christ removes the very shadow it casts.

How joyful is the one
whose transgression is forgiven,
whose sin is covered!
How joyful is a person whom
the LORD does not charge with iniquity
and in whose spirit is no deceit!

When I kept silent, my bones became brittle
from my groaning all day long.
For day and night your hand was heavy on me;
my strength was drained
as in the summer's heat.
Then I acknowledged my sin to you
and did not conceal my iniquity.
I said, "I will confess my transgressions to the LORD,"
and you forgave the guilt of my sin. (Psalm 32:1-5)

Judah's Turn

REPENTING OF SIN

As soon as the story of repentance and reconciliation in the lives of Joseph and his brothers started, it seemed to grind to a halt. The brothers were stuck in Canaan, unable to return to Egypt to get Simeon without Jacob allowing Benjamin to go with them. We don't know how long they stayed away, but I am sure that for Joseph the wait was agonizing.

Where are you in your own story? Do you feel stuck, the words "I forgive you" impossible to say or hear? Joseph's family was stuck too—until they became unstuck through an unexpected catalyst.

The story of Joseph is a model to all of us. For while it tells the story of one sinned against, it also tells the story of one who sinned.

JUDAH

> *The scepter will not depart from Judah or the staff from between his feet until he whose right it is comes and the obedience of the peoples belongs to him. (Genesis 49:10)*

Even if you don't know much of Scripture, you will likely

have heard the name Judah. There's the tribe of Judah; Jesus is the Lion of Judah. The name Judah in Scripture is honored. It is stunning, then, to read of the brutal, self-serving man in Genesis 37 and 38 from whose line the Savior of the world would eventually be born.

Judah was Jacob's fourth son, born to him by the wife Jacob had been tricked into marrying. Earlier chapters of Genesis tell stories about Judah's older brothers, but Judah himself isn't mentioned beyond his birth until he speaks up in Genesis 37 with the idea of selling Joseph into slavery. The next chapters of Genesis give us contrasting details of both Joseph's and Judah's lives—one lived in slavery to others; the other lived serving only himself. While Joseph was remaining faithful to God even in captivity in Potiphar's house, Judah was raising sons who were so offensive to God that God put two of them to death. While Joseph was resisting solicitations for sex by Potiphar's wife, Judah was paying a prostitute for sex—a woman who turned out to be his own daughter-in-law. The contrast is jarring.

The apostle Paul's great summary of our sinful condition in Ephesians 2 gives us language for the state we first find Judah in:

> *You were dead in your trespasses and sins ... We too all previously lived among them in our fleshly desires, carrying out the inclinations of our flesh and thoughts, and we were by nature children under wrath. (Ephesians 2:1-3)*

Judah, in Genesis 37, was the walking representation of a person dead to God and alive only to his own whims and desires. His nature was to do what he wanted, when he wanted, without care for the cost to others.

After Judah had the idea of selling Joseph into slavery, he went on with his life. But his family was deeply dysfunctional. After his oldest two sons died because of great evil they did against God, Judah sent his widowed daughter-in-law, Tamar, away without any provision for her inheritance in his family. Tamar devised a plan to get pregnant by Judah so that she would have the heir in the family she needed. She dressed as a prostitute and waited for Judah by the side of a road. Her plan worked.

Three months after Judah had sex with the woman he thought was an unknown prostitute, he learned that Tamar was pregnant. In the climactic scene of Genesis 38, Judah called, "Bring her out, and let her be burned to death!" (v 24) But Tamar had executed her plan well. She sent her father-in-law a message: "I am pregnant by the man to whom these items belong" (v 25). With her message were Judah's own signet ring, cord, and staff—the things he had left with her when he thought she was a prostitute.

I can imagine Judah, caught up in his self-righteous vengeance, staring at his own signet ring as it dawned on him that it was Tamar who had been dressed up as the prostitute along the road. He himself was the father of her child. He himself had set her up for this situation by his refusal to do right by her after the death of her husband, his own wicked son.

"She is more righteous than I," Judah admitted (v 26). I imagine the confused silence, then growing whispers, of the crowd that had gathered to see Tamar burned. Judah's words must have stunned them all. Tamar was spared, and Judah was humbled. Her twin sons would be Judah's heirs—named in the lineage of Christ in Matthew 1 and Luke 3.

Judah, dead in his sin, was beginning to stir in his grave.

A BROTHER'S KEEPER

By Genesis 43, Judah was no longer a man in charge of his own destiny, answering only to his own whims. After being humbled by his interaction with Tamar, he had been further broken by the famine that took away his ability to provide for his family.

He had learned the fragility of his own freedom when Joseph had held him with his other brothers in custody for three days. There, as we saw, he and his brothers had been stirred awake to the horror of their sin against Joseph. The grace of God, the unnamed actor moving this story toward reconciliation, was at work in Judah's life, stirring in his heart, moving him from death to life.

Now Jacob's family in Canaan was on the verge of starvation a second time. The food the brothers had brought back from Egypt was eventually used up by their large family, and the famine remained severe. Despite their fear that they would be imprisoned for not paying for the grain the first time, and despite Jacob's reluctance to let Benjamin go, the brothers knew that to survive, they had no choice but to return to Egypt once again.

Joseph had told them on their first trip that they had to bring their little brother back to prove they weren't spies. There would be no food for them a second time without bringing Benjamin. As we've seen, it was an agonizing choice for Jacob, who had already lost so much that was precious to him.

Would Jacob's family starve to death or would he allow his youngest son to go in an effort to get food? As Jacob wrestled with his grief, Judah stepped up with words that were totally at odds with the person he had shown himself to be in Genesis 37 and 38.

> *Then Judah said to his father Israel, "Send the boy with*
> *me. We will be on our way so that we may live and*
> *not die—neither we, nor you, nor our dependents. I*
> *will be responsible for him. You can hold me personally*
> *accountable! If I do not bring him back to you and set him*
> *before you, I will be guilty before you forever.*
>
> *(Genesis 43:8-9)*

"

The grace of God, the unnamed actor moving this story toward reconciliation, was stirring Judah's heart.

"

This was a complete turnaround from the actions of the man we met in Genesis 37 and 38. Judah had been responsible for the welfare of Joseph, but he had sold his brother into a lifetime of slavery. Then he had been responsible for the welfare of Tamar, but he had cut her off from support and even called for her to be burned to death. In both cases, he had served only himself, at the expense of the ones he was called to protect. He had casually disregarded his own family members. But now, he took responsibility for Benjamin's life. He put his life and welfare on the line for Benjamin's—and for the wider family. This was a profound change. Judah was turning from his sinful ways. Judah had begun to repent.

MORE THAN REGRET

The English word *repent* comes from the Latin for "regret." But the Bible presents the concept as more than just regret. It is more than simply feeling bad about something you have done. Nowhere is this distinction between simple regret and genuine repentance laid out more clearly than by the apostle Paul in his second letter to believers at the church in Corinth.

In a previous letter, he had confronted the church in clear terms for their sins against him and God. That letter upset the believers that read it. Paul responded in 2 Corinthians 7:9-10:

> *I now rejoice, not because you were grieved, but because your grief led to repentance. For you were grieved as God willed, so that you didn't experience any loss from us. For godly grief produces a repentance that leads to salvation without regret, but worldly grief produces death.*

Paul drew a line between what he called "worldly grief" and "godly grief" over sin. Godly grief produced repentance, Paul said. The Greek word Paul used for repentance was *metanoia*, which literally means changing one's mind. It means thinking differently about your sin.

The closest Old Testament equivalent to *metanoia* is the Hebrew word *shuwb*, which means to turn or return. 1 Kings 13:33 provides a clear example of this word. After prophets had warned Israel's idolatrous King Jeroboam of the consequences of his sin of idolatry, we are told:

> *Even after this, Jeroboam did not repent of his evil way but again made priests for the high places from the ranks of the people.*

Whether or not Jeroboam felt "worldly grief" over the consequences of his sin, he certainly didn't repent. He didn't change his mind. He didn't turn from his evil ways but continued on in the same direction, embracing and promoting idol worship.

The apostle Paul further reinforces the connection between repentance and turning in Acts 26:20:

> *Instead, I preached … that they should repent and turn to God, and do works worthy of repentance.*

Repentance in the Bible, then, is more than feeling regret. Repentance is regret that turns away from the sin and walks forward in the opposite direction.

A person has repented when they recognize that the thing they once thought was ok was definitely not ok, and they turn from it.

We have repented when we say out loud that the thing we thought wouldn't hurt anyone and was nobody else's business actually did hurt others and was their business.

We have repented when we acknowledge that the act we thought would be good, even though God said it was sin, actually harmed ourselves and others.

We have repented when we admit that we have participated in a system that has harmed others and make changes to no longer participate in it.

When Judah took responsibility and accountability for Benjamin before his dad, he acted in a way that, as Paul said, was "worthy of repentance." That act showed that his heart and mind had changed. Like Joseph before him, Benjamin was now the favored son. But Judah no longer hated him. He no longer saw sending the favored son to Egypt as a convenient way to get ahead in the family but as a horrible thing that would destroy the family. He was no longer willing to sacrifice another's life to secure his own self-interest. Instead, he put his own life and inheritance on the line. He would protect Benjamin. He would be accountable for Benjamin. He had radically and wholeheartedly changed his mind and direction.

CIRCLING IN PLACE

Have you recognized your sin and turned from it? Or would you recognize if the one who harmed you truly repented? We may look for the specific words "I repent." But repentance isn't demonstrated by those words. It's demonstrated by a turning away from sin.

On the road to reconciliation, it is necessary to sit for a time in the roundabout of repentance, circling in place until we are ready to drive out in a completely different direction. It is not enough to simply recognize our offense against God and others. It is not enough to regret our actions. It is not enough to feel bad about how things turned out. Repentance is more than saying, "I'm sorry." It's more than admitting our guilt. The roundabout of repentance is the place where we lay down our self-justification, acknowledge what we have done, and turn away from it. The roundabout of repentance sends us out from its circle in an entirely new direction. Now we do good works in contrast with the wrong we used to do.

Are there wrongs you have done that broke relationship with another? What is the opposite of that sin? If you are the one who caused the breach, what can you practically do to demonstrate you are on a new path?

The apostle Paul gives some specifics in his letter to the church at Ephesus:

> *Therefore, putting away lying, speak the truth, each one to his neighbor ... Let the thief no longer steal. Instead, he is to do honest work with his own hands, so that he has something to share with anyone in need. No foul language should come from your mouth, but only what is good for building up someone in need, so that it gives grace to those who hear.* (Ephesians 4:25, 28-29)

Did you lie? Repentance means you now speak truth. Did you steal? Repentance means you now do honest work that you can share with others. Did you gossip maliciously or tear down others with your speech? Repentance means you now speak words that build up and give grace.

God's kindness, as Paul told believers in Romans 2:4, draws us to repent. If repentance and turning from sin feel impossible to you, know that this very kind of change—seen in the stories of Judah, of the Samaritan woman at the well, of the murderous Saul who became the apostle Paul—is exactly what Jesus came to accomplish for us all. Repentance and genuine change are possible through God's grace to us.

WAITING ON REPENTANCE

What if you are still waiting for someone to repent of the harm they have done? Maybe they paint you as the problem—the one who brought the conflict on yourself. They take no responsibility for their actions against you or they do not acknowledge the cost of their actions in your life. Maybe, after years of waiting, your only instinct in any interaction with them is simply to protect yourself or your loved ones from future harm.

Or maybe the one who harmed you only experiences regret. Maybe they are sorry that their relationship with you has been broken. But they haven't truly repented. They haven't realized that the actions against you which they justified for a time were actually wrong and harmful. They haven't changed their mind about what they did to you or others. You have experienced this person more as Judah in Genesis 37 and 38 than Judah in the later chapters of Joseph's story.

When your opponent has sinned against you, harmed you or your loved ones, justified their actions against you, and nothing more, it is hard to believe they could ever change. Abuse masks the humanity of the abuser. As a result, it is hard for those who wait for repentance to remember their opponent's humanity and treat them as image-bearers of God—as those in whom God can produce repentance.

Judah's actions were inhumane toward both Joseph and Tamar. He treated both Joseph and Tamar as less than human. But Judah acted as less than human too. In the animal kingdom, "survival of the fittest" rules the world. But humankind, made in the image of God, has a particular characteristic that sets them apart from animals. They are humane—they show compassion or benevolence in a way animals cannot.

After the fall, inhumanity, not humanity, ruled the day. Cain killed Abel. A beastly type of survival of the fittest ruled the world outside of Eden. Civilization was not very civilized until God's law broke into this world. God legislated the humane treatment of one another on Mount Sinai. *Do not kill. Do not steal. Love God. Love your neighbor. Act like image-bearers of me,* God instructed. In his law, God called us back to benevolence and compassion. Humankind, made in the image of God, should treat others humanely.

What happened when you found yourself in a situation in which compassion and benevolence did not rule the day? You were not treated with the inherent dignity due to an image-bearer of God. By treating you that way, your oppressor did not act as an image-bearer of God either. As time goes on without repentance, it is hard to treat humanely the one who acted against you. We harden our heart. Often that seems to be the only way to survive mentally.

But the story of Judah calls us to hope for our opponent's repentance. It reminds us that God can bring to life the most inhumane opponent. God calls our opponent to image him out in the world, just as he calls us. Do we hope for that for them? Or have we written them off as less than human? This is a crossroads of faith for any of us who wait for someone to repent.

In 2 Timothy 2:24-26, Paul gives important instructions for anyone waiting for their opponent to repent:

The Lord's servant must not quarrel, but must be gentle to everyone, able to teach, and patient, instructing his opponents with gentleness. Perhaps God will grant them repentance leading them to the knowledge of the truth. Then they may come to their senses and escape the trap of the devil, who has taken them captive to do his will.

Paul reminded Timothy of a key thing—our opponent is trapped in their sin by Satan! This insight into our opponent's condition helps us treat them humanely, with compassion for them as captives of the enemy of all humankind. This truth enables us to pray and hope for our opponent that God would "grant them repentance" that opens their eyes to their condition and leads them "to the knowledge of the truth."

Judah's transformation gives me such hope for my opponent. The godless, inhumane man from Genesis 37 and 38 became someone who laid down his rights for another in Genesis 43 and 44. He was the opponent taken captive by Satan who was granted repentance by God. Joseph's interactions with Judah model Paul's instructions in 2 Timothy 2. Joseph was gentle. He kept his strength under control. But don't mistake his gentleness for weakness! A baby is weak. A parent is gentle. Adults have the strength to crush their infant, but they temper that strength to instead cradle and protect their child. Joseph too had the power to crush Judah, but he tempered that strength and treated him gently, hoping for change.

After Judah's sacrificial commitment to his father for Benjamin's welfare, Jacob relented. "If I am deprived of my sons, then I am deprived," he said (Genesis 43:14). The stage was now set for the brothers to return to Egypt. After months in limbo, Joseph and his brothers were finally unstuck. They were moving forward again toward reconciliation—though none of them realized it at the time.

The Lord does not delay his promise, as some understand delay, but is patient with you, not wanting any to perish but all to come to repentance. (2 Peter 3:9)

Amazing 6 Grace

FORGIVING THE DEBT

Six years after the original church conflict first harmed my family and many others, the tide seemed to turn. Though the pastor of our megachurch never recognized the harm he had done or repented of his angry responses, other elders and their wives began to recognize their offenses and specifically name them with individuals they had harmed.

I remember when one former elder, Tom, first called me. Tom and Diane (not their real names) had been our community-group leaders. They had hosted our family for many Thanksgivings, and Diane had organized my baby showers. They had been dear friends—right up to the moment the lead pastor fired two elders and threw the church into a conflict from which it would never recover. Then they never spoke to us again—until Tom's name showed up in my caller ID.

Shunning and ostracism had been the primary tools used by pastors and elders and their wives at the megachurch to punish those who disagreed with the firing of the two older elders who had meant so much to us. I had three friends in particular whose primary friendship groups at church were elders and their wives. When they saw the same problems in the conflict that I did, each was immediately cut off.

I will never forget the conversation I had with the eight-year-old son of one such couple. He told me, "We used to go to the park with [the pastor's family] all the time. But now I never see them. It just stopped." It was a heartbreaking conversation. Shunning is a simple but effective tactic with devastating mental results. It had done much harm to both adults and children in the aftermath of this church conflict.

I was so stunned that Tom was calling me that I didn't answer the phone. He left a message, which I listened to multiple times. Much like Judah in Genesis 43, Tom had been humbled by his own circumstances. He had lost his job. His family was in crisis. His own experiences in the church that past year had brought clarity on how he had harmed others. He was vulnerable and humble as he approached me. But I too was vulnerable. The losses from that conflict remained painful in my life. I did not want to open myself to more hurt.

But the path toward reconciliation is not for those who want to avoid pain. It is for those willing to walk through the pain, believing that God has called us to something better than our status quo of broken relationship. I called Tom back. In our phone call, he named his sin and the harm done to those the elders had either fired or alienated. We set up a time for me to talk to Diane in person as well. She too clearly articulated the harm she had participated in.

Tom and Diane began the hard work of reconciling with those harmed by their part in that church conflict years before. Often, they were met with suspicion by those they had harmed. Reconciliation didn't happen in a single conversation. It didn't for Joseph and his brothers either.

We have reached a pivotal moment in Joseph's story. In Genesis 43, his brothers were trying to do the right thing—the necessary thing—for the survival of their family.

"

The path to reconciliation
is for those willing to walk
through the pain, believing
God has something better.

"

They were trying to do the right thing by their father. They were trying to do the right thing by their little brother, Benjamin. And they were trying to do the right thing by the prime minister of Egypt, to whom (as they thought) they still owed money for the food they had brought home the first time.

Yet the right thing—the necessary thing—put them in a vulnerable position with Joseph. When Tom and Diane approached me to ask for forgiveness, it put them in a vulnerable position as well. I could have rejected them or shamed them. I could have refused to forgive them. I could have made a public spectacle of them. They were risking themselves when they approached me.

Asking for forgiveness means making yourself vulnerable. Offering forgiveness does too. Yet as we'll see in this chapter, taking the step of forgiveness is vital if we are to move forward at all.

BACK TO EGYPT

Joseph's brothers were still living with the guilt of how they had harmed Joseph years before. When they first discovered that the money intended to pay for the grain on their first trip had been returned to them, "their hearts sank" (Genesis 42:28). Trembling, they wondered, "What has God done to us?" They thought the mysterious return of the silver—which could only be interpreted as stealing from the prime minister—was God's way of punishing them for all they had taken from Joseph in his youth. This fear of God's vengeance had hung over their heads for months.

But starvation proved a harsher taskmaster for Jacob's family than their fear of Joseph. When the brothers arrived in Egypt the second time—now with Benjamin in tow—they were quickly taken to Joseph's house. Imagine the ice-cold dread that descended over their hearts. This was it—their judgment day. As they entered Joseph's house, Judah and his brothers were breaking under the multiple weights of stress and guilt they were carrying. They were fully at Joseph's mercy, and they knew they deserved wrath.

> *They said, "We have been brought here because of the silver that was returned in our bags the first time. They intend to overpower us, seize us, make us slaves, and take our donkeys." (Genesis 43:18)*

Joseph's brothers were convinced that the Egyptians were going to make them all prisoners. They knew how easy it was for the powerful to make the vulnerable into slaves—they had done it to their own brother. Would Jacob now be left with no sons at all? Would the rest of their family starve to death in Canaan? All their fears seemed to be coming true. God was going to use the Egyptians to exact punishment on them for their treatment of Joseph.

The brothers approached Joseph's steward when they arrived and quickly admitted that the money had been returned to them on their previous trip. "We have brought additional silver with us," they explained anxiously. "We don't know who put the silver in the bags" (Genesis 43:22).

But Joseph's steward stunned them with his reply.

> *Don't be afraid. Your God and the God of your father must have put treasure in your bags. I received your silver. (v 23)*

Joseph's steward didn't just relieve the brothers of months of anxiety. He also made a bold claim. The very God that the brothers had expected to exact vengeance upon them was the one who had restored their treasure to them. This Egyptian wasn't speaking about his own religion but of Abraham's, Isaac's, and Jacob's. He wasn't talking about Egyptian gods but the true God, Yahweh. The steward wasn't speaking generally nice words to the brothers but words of grace specific to their family in the context of their own beliefs.

The steward then brought Simeon out to them. Instead of imprisoning the brothers as they expected, he set Simeon free. Instead of exacting judgment for the grain they had taken without payment, he assured them it was a gift from their God.

FORGIVENESS
What is forgiveness, as the Bible uses the word? The New Testament word, *aphiemi*, means to let go or give up a debt.

And forgive us our debts, as we also have forgiven our debtors. (Matthew 6:12)

It's a financial term. When a lender makes a choice to release a borrower from repaying their debt in full, the borrower has been forgiven their debt. Forgiveness is the release by a creditor of any expectation that a debt will be repaid. Joseph modeled the literal sense of *aphiemi* when he returned his brothers' silver and provided grain for them without payment.

Who eats the cost when a debt is forgiven? The offended party. They absorb the loss. Forgiveness is fundamentally lopsided. The debtor gains, and the creditor loses.

Joseph lost. He lost money. But more than that, in setting his brothers free, he lost his opportunity to gain compensation for all those years he had spent without his dad and little brother. Forgiveness is an act of sacrifice—a willingness to take the loss without retaliation. And it is radically offensive to a world that cries out for retribution.

WRATH DISMANTLED
In June of 2015, breaking news took over my TV screen as night fell on my house in Seattle. Blue lights of patrol cars blinked in the dark behind the reporter outside a stark white church in downtown Charleston, South Carolina. There had been a shooting at the evening Bible study of Emanuel AME Church. I was stunned, my heart ice cold, as I witnessed the

horror unfolding a mere hour and a half from my hometown in South Carolina—to which I was moving in one month's time. Dylann Roof, a young white supremacist, had killed nine black church members during their Wednesday evening Bible study. It is impossible to put into words the terror which that event brought to black families in my hometown community. It was the most horrible, grievous thing I had ever seen. That one act encapsulated to me all that was wrong in the world.

48 hours after the killings, Roof made his first appearance in court. Nadine Collier, daughter of murder victim Ethel Lance, was first to speak.

> *I forgive you ... You took something really precious from me. I will never talk to her ever again, I will never be able to hold her again, but I forgive you and have mercy on your soul.*[1]

Several other family members of those killed uttered similar words. It shocked the world. Many were amazed. Many were offended. Didn't such words let white supremacists off the hook? Moral outrage, not Christian grace, seemed the most effective way of keeping the spotlight on the injustices that black folks in our community still experience daily. Commenting on the hearing some years later, Philip Pinckney, a black pastor of a cross-cultural church in Charleston, gave voice to the struggle that many had:

> *At first glance, forgiveness seems like it's giving people a way out of repentance and out of a hard conversation ... Many ... see [forgiveness] as weakness rather than being helpful.*[2]

---

1 www.usatoday.com/story/life/movies/2019/06/17/emanuel-explores-power-for-giveness-after-charleston-church-massacre/1478473001 (accessed June 23, 2021).

2 www.christianitytoday.com/ct/2019/june-web-only/emmanuel-charleston-docu-mentary-racial-justice-forgiveness.html (accessed June 23, 2021).

Nadine Collier's forgiveness of Dylann Roof should not be confused with cheap grace, a term coined by Dietrich Bonhoeffer, a Christian martyred by the Nazis in World War II. Cheap grace, as Bonhoeffer used the term, is the pretense that we can have forgiveness for free—it is grace without the cross, grace without cost. God does not extend grace to us without sending Jesus to the cross and requiring us to respond in faith and repentance. Likewise, if our words of forgiveness communicate that everything is ok—that the wrong done doesn't really matter—we have lost the meaning of the word "grace" as the Bible uses it. If our gracious responses carry the expectation that folks will go on as they always did, we are bartering with cheap, imitation grace. And it will not get us far.

Desmond Tutu and his daughter Mpho, who endured grave racial injustice under apartheid in South Africa, illustrate this distinction in *The Book of Forgiving*. Forgiveness is not weakness, it is not forgetting, and it does not subvert true justice. Instead, forgiveness "creates space for justice to be enacted with a purity of purpose that does not include revenge" (p 40).

I said in the last chapter that abuse masks the humanity of the abuser. When Nadine Collier forgave Dylann Roof, she called him back from his monstrous acts and reminded him of his humanity. By treating him with grace, she implicitly called him to account for his horrible acts, which had hurt so many. What she did not do was pretend that Roof's harm was anything less than what it was.

Roof would still receive his sentence and be justly punished for what he had done. But when family members spoke of forgiveness to Roof, they let go of the debt that he owed them. It was one he could never repay anyway—what compensation could there be for the loss of a loved one? Those who forgave Roof also let go of the opportunity for any satisfaction that letting out their anger against him in a public hearing might have temporarily gained for them. They treated him in a way he didn't deserve, a way he had not treated their loved ones.

No one was forgiving racism as an idea, Brian Ivie, the director of the documentary *Emanuel* on the Charleston Nine, explains:

Their heart is to forgive this person, who is still a human being and who we all hope will be redeemed.[3]

Such forgiveness is offensive to many people. We need to own that reality. Forgiveness costs the one who forgives, not the one who harmed. It costs them the satisfaction of retribution. It costs them the possibility of recouping their losses. It is lopsided. It is not fair. But it is godly.

I now live about 90 minutes away from Emanuel AME Church. I have driven by it many times and stopped there to pray on more than one occasion. The forgiveness offered by the families of those murdered did not let our community off the hook. It did not let us pretend that the wrong did not happen. It did not pave the way for our community to ignore the legacy of white supremacy in our state. Forgiveness did not brush over the harm that was done: it acknowledged it, grieved it, and provoked change.

Chris Singleton, whose mother was killed by Roof, noted that Roof had set out to start a race war. When he forgave Roof, Singleton helped dismantle the ticking time bomb that Roof had tried to ignite. Chris said he found great comfort personally in the fact that the community, which had lost so much, reacted in the opposite way to what Roof intended. Their forgiveness thwarted Roof's ultimate goal of provoking mass conflict in the region.

---

3 www.christianitytoday.com/ct/2019/june-web-only/emmanuel-charleston-documentary-racial-justice-forgiveness.html (accessed June 23, 2021).

BETTER THAN REVENGE

While revenge movies often show the avenger walking away strong and tall, going about their business after they've dealt retribution on the bad guy, that isn't how it works in real life. Revenge doesn't satisfy the deep vulnerability in our hearts and minds caused by our wounds. We may act out angrily in response to the harm done to us or to our loved ones, but revenge cannot fix our pain.

The Spirit spoke wisdom to us when he inspired the apostle Paul to write:

> *Do not repay anyone evil for evil. Give careful thought to do what is honorable in everyone's eyes. If possible, as far as it depends on you, live at peace with everyone. Friends, do not avenge yourselves; instead, leave room for God's wrath, because it is written, Vengeance belongs to me; I will repay, says the Lord. (Romans 12:17-19)*

In these commands, God asks us to trust him to bring perfect justice, just as we trust him in the way he dealt with our own sin at the cross. So, we forgive because he first forgave us and because he asks us to forgive others. But we also forgive because it is good for us. God created humankind. He knows our psyche better than anyone, and it was his love for us that prompted him to guide us in this way. *Do not avenge yourselves. Leave that to God.* Our bodies and minds cannot sustain long-term bitterness and anger without deep damage to our own inner selves. Grief over our wounds is painful, but anger over them harms us even more.

Does your anger at the one who harmed you or your loved one seethe as an undercurrent of your life? I spent a lot of time yelling at my bathroom mirror all the things I would say to the pastor whose own anger problems had devastated our church family. My frustration over what he had done and my inability to get him to correct the harm were debilitating for a while—an undercurrent of poison in my life. It was unhealthy for me, and it was unhealthy for those around me.

In *The Book of Forgiving*, the Tutus point out scientific studies that show the relationship between physical stress and a lack of forgiveness. Holding on to our anger can harm us physically as well as emotionally. Failure to forgive can increase our risk for heart disease, high blood pressure, and other stress-related illnesses. Lack of forgiveness keeps us tied to the one who has wronged us, tethered by chains of bitterness. Our offender becomes our jailor.

When we forgive, "we become our own liberators" (Tutu, *The Book of Forgiving*, p 16). The offenses of the other person no longer control our responses. We may still live with the consequences of the harm done to us in the past, but we do not allow that harm to cloud our future.

IS FORGIVENESS POSSIBLE?

Despite all of the arguments one could make for why forgiveness is good and healthy, the real question for anyone who has endured great harm from another is much simpler. Is forgiveness even possible? How do we forgive one who has taken much from us? Philip Pinckney said it well: "Without a Holy Spirit renewed mind, [forgiveness] is not going to make sense."

We have already seen that recalling the humanity of the perpetrator is key to forgiving them. But we also need a truly biblical understanding of what our shared humanity means. We are all divine image-bearers, but we are all also sinners. Under the right pressures and influences, all of us are capable of harming others. Understanding our own propensity toward sin is necessary to move away from retribution against our enemy toward forgiveness.

We too all previously lived among them in our fleshly desires, carrying out the inclinations of our flesh and thoughts, and we were by nature children under wrath as the others were also. But God, who is rich in mercy, because of his great love that he had for us, made us alive with Christ even though we were dead in trespasses. You are saved by grace! (Ephesians 2:3-5)

Paul taught that all of us, by our very nature, deserve God's wrath. But God's mercy and love toward us were great. We were dead in our sins when he made us alive through Jesus Christ.

I, too, given the right circumstances and influences, am capable of great evil. I was not saved by my inherent worthiness of salvation but by God's great love and mercy for me. I am saved by his grace. This is the foundation for my ability to turn toward my oppressor with forgiveness: the forgiveness and grace that God has shown me.

Forgiveness is a supernatural act that we could never do in our own strength. True forgiveness requires the Holy Spirit to empower us to do what would otherwise be impossible. Who except someone with the Holy Spirit's indwelling power could offer Dylann Roof forgiveness for murdering their loved one? Roof's victims were devout believers, and many of those who were left to mourn them were as well. That old, white-painted church on Calhoun Street in Charleston, founded because of the white supremacy that denied black people a full seat at the Lord's table, stands as a symbol of Christ's forgiveness, of grace in the face of evil.

Those who forgave Roof did not thwart justice, but they allowed, as the Tutus phrase it, a pure pursuit of justice not tainted by revenge. While their words of forgiveness calmed tensions around Charleston, they also convicted of sin. Their forgiveness did not sweep sin under the carpet. Their forgiveness did not excuse Roof's actions. There was no way around the honest accounting of the debt Roof owed. Their forgiveness acknowledged the real offense that had to be forgiven, but it also called a community to see the one who had harmed them as a person, not solely as his offense.

Have you resisted forgiving another because you are afraid it minimizes the harm they have done? I cannot guarantee that the one you forgive will understand what it cost you to do so. There is no indication that Dylann Roof did. But our forgiveness of others isn't fundamentally about them. It doesn't flow from how they have responded to their sin against us. It flows from how God has responded to our sins against him.

Forgiveness requires us to account for the mercy we have received from God—a grace that is not cheap but required the death of his Son on the cross. And then it chooses to offer mercy over revenge to the one who offended us. God equips each of us, through his great love and mercy toward us and the grace upon grace of his Holy Spirit living in us, to extend that mercy toward others. It is stunning to others when we do, because it is supernatural. It is not of this world.

AMAZING GRACE

Imagine the shock felt by Judah and the other brothers as they heard the words of Joseph's steward. Their debt had been paid! They did not owe for the grain they had received. They did not owe for the additional supplies Joseph had sent with them (Genesis 42:25). It had all been a gift, freely given, with no strings attached.

Their shock continued as Joseph's steward brought them inside, gave them water, and washed their feet. Did they whisper to each other behind his back as they tried to understand what was happening? His hospitality to them was stunning after the months of fear they had felt over the returned silver. The steward fed their animals and started to prepare a meal for the brothers. Somehow they had found themselves being invited to a feast in the house of the prime minister of Egypt.

When Joseph arrived, the brothers, still nervous, offered him gifts and bowed to the ground before him. Joseph spoke kindly to them and inquired about their father.

When Joseph spotted Benjamin for the first time, he proclaimed, "May God be gracious to you, my son." Then, all at once, he rushed out of the room to weep privately. Joseph was still vulnerable. He still bore great hurt. His grace to his brothers had not undone his pain—but neither did his pain and vulnerability keep him from offering them grace.

These gestures from Joseph were the exact opposite of what one would expect from someone sold into slavery by the ones he now fed and sheltered. At this point in Joseph's story, the brothers didn't understand exactly what was happening. They didn't know why Joseph was treating them this way. But they did know that the vengeance they had expected from God had turned out to be grace. Now they were eating at the table of the one they thought they had offended. They were experiencing the firstfruits of the forgiveness Joseph was ready to offer them. The brothers ate, drank, and were merry at Joseph's table that night.

The men looked at each other in astonishment.

(Genesis 43:33)

Forgiveness is shocking. It's utterly amazing. It's amazing to the one receiving forgiveness when they know they deserve wrath. And it's amazing to those of us who witness it from the sidelines. A whole nation was amazed—stunned actually— to watch humble Christians from Charleston on national television speaking words of profound mercy to the face of one who had committed unspeakable evil against them. Nothing but Christian *aphiemi* empowered by Christ's own forgiveness on the cross could have stopped the snowball of evil Roof had set rolling. The families of the Charleston Nine stopped evil in its tracks. Why? Because Jesus had done the same for them first.

Just as the Lord has forgiven you, so you are also to forgive.
                                                    (Colossians 3:13)

Foundation Work

REPAIRING THE DAMAGE

Several years ago, I remodeled my grandparents' farmhouse—the one in which my mother was raised. The ancient paned windows from the 1930s were painted shut. The sheetrock, installed in the 1960s, was full of mold. Underneath it, the walls were filled with mouse nests and droppings. And the kitchen cabinets hung crooked. But before anything else could be repaired, the builders had to strip back layer after layer of linoleum from the kitchen floor. Underneath it was the root problem that had to be fixed before other, more cosmetic work could begin. The foundation under the kitchen had rotted. Until that was fixed, any other work done on the house was destined to fail long term. The foundation had to be repaired.

Isn't it the same in human relationships? You can apologize for a bitter response to your spouse, but you'll respond the same way again and again until you deal with the underlying wound of their abusive words or past unfaithfulness. You can start getting to know a parent who wasn't around in your childhood, but, at some point, you will have to deal with the pain of their abandonment of you as a child. We can spackle and paint over cracks in the walls of our relationships, but until the foundation is repaired, those cracks will inevitably show themselves again.

Not every relationship will reach reconciliation. It is possible to forgive those who do not see their need to be forgiven. It is possible to let go of our need for revenge or payback and release the debt owed to us by the one who harmed us. But full reconciliation requires more.

The work of reconciliation is a two-way street: neither the offender nor the one harmed can bear all of it. The weight of forgiveness, discussed in the last chapter, lies on the shoulders of the one who was harmed. But the weight of repairing the wrong lies on the shoulders of the one who did the harm. It may well be that you are not the one who did the harm—at least, not in the situation that made you pick up this book. "It's the person who wronged me who really needs to read this chapter!" you might be thinking. But keep reading. It is helpful to think through what needs to be repaired, even if you are not the one who needs to repair it. And my own experience has taught me that even as we wait for the foundation work to be done by the one who wronged us, God can open our eyes to harm done in other places—damage that *is* ours to deal with.

SAVING A BROTHER

After 22 years in Egypt, Joseph was now finally reunited with the brothers who had sold him into slavery. But he had not yet revealed to them his identity. He wanted to be reconciled with his family, but the offenses against him still cut deeply. It would take more than his forgiveness to repair their relationship. Joseph had overheard his brothers acknowledge their sin against him, but he needed to know, once for all, if there had been a true change in their hearts from the callous, calculating, and cruel brothers he had known as a teenager. Could the foundation of their broken relationship be repaired? To find out, Joseph devised a final test for his brothers that was tied directly to their sin against him.

After their astonishment at Joseph's mercy and the night of drunken merriment in his house, the brothers prepared to return to their father in Canaan with more grain to sustain their family. Unbeknown to them, Joseph directed his steward to once again return their silver with the food. But this time, he told him to plant Joseph's own silver cup in Benjamin's bag.

The brothers had not made it far out of Egypt when Joseph's men caught up with their caravan. "Why have you repaid evil for good?" were their harsh words of accusation (Genesis 44:4). What new calamity was this? Whatever previous relief the brothers had felt at Joseph's table was crushed under these stunning new accusations. The brothers denied any wrongdoing, but, sure enough, Joseph's silver cup was found in Benjamin's bag. The brothers were shocked and horrified.

Joseph's steward demanded that Benjamin return to be Joseph's slave. Here was the test. Would the brothers jump at this chance to get rid of their father's favored son, as they had done when the same opportunity arose with Joseph years before? Did the brothers harbor the same jealousy against Benjamin that they had held in Genesis 37 against Joseph? This time, if they let Benjamin be taken, they would have a legitimate excuse for his loss.

But instead of devising how to use these events to get rid of another favored son, Judah and his brothers tore their clothes in torment. Instead of sending Benjamin alone to Egypt as they had done with Joseph, the brothers returned to Egypt with him.

When the brothers reached Egypt and stood before Joseph, it was Judah, once again, who stepped up.

"What can we say to my lord?" Judah replied. "How can we plead? How can we justify ourselves? God has exposed your servants' iniquity. We are now my lord's slaves—both we and the one in whose possession the cup was found."

(Genesis 44:16)

Judah was undone. He threw himself on Joseph's mercy. But he didn't plead Benjamin's innocence. Instead, he acknowledged the brothers' guilt. Judah may not have deserved to be punished over that particular cup found in Benjamin's bag, but he knew all too well that he indeed bore guilt for a serious crime. He had hated his little brother Joseph and sold him into slavery. With his brothers, he had faked Joseph's death and brought his coat, soaked in the blood of an animal, to their father. He had robbed Joseph of his family and prosperity. He had denied him his possession in the land. His debt to Joseph was incalculable. He could not justify himself before the man he knew only as prime minister of Egypt after all that lay on his conscience from his sins against Joseph. The God of their fathers had returned their money the first time, but it seemed he was requiring just punishment now.

It would have been easy for Judah to do to Benjamin as he had done to Joseph. After all, Benjamin had apparently stolen this man's silver cup. He would get what he deserved. But Judah demonstrated once again that he had changed. When Joseph reiterated his desire to keep Benjamin as his slave, Judah responded again with words totally at odds with the person he had shown himself to be in Genesis 37 and 38.

Now please let your servant remain here as my lord's slave, in place of the boy. Let him go back with his brothers. For how can I go back to my father without the boy? I could not bear to see the grief that would overwhelm my father.

(Genesis 44:33-34)

This was the moment when the truth of Judah's heart was fully exposed to Joseph. Instead of sacrificing his brother because he was jealous of his father's favoritism, and instead of callously serving his own interests over those of his family, Judah offered himself in his brother's place. He didn't realize it at the time, but he had begun to repair at a foundational level the damage his sin had caused.

Judah could not undo the wrong of stealing Joseph's freedom. But by offering himself in place of Benjamin, he had begun to repair the deep wound in Joseph's heart.

COMPELLED TO REPAY

God had transformed Judah's heart. He loved his father and could not bear to see him overwhelmed again with grief. The selfish man was now selfless. The faithless man was now trustworthy, keeping his word to his father to protect Benjamin at all costs. The young man full of hate and bitterness who sold his younger brother for his own personal benefit was now willing to give his own life in servitude to save his little brother. This was no papering over cracks. Judah had changed at a foundational level.

We too need a heart changed by God to pursue full reconciliation with those whom we have offended and sinned against. Most of the time, people only repair the cracks. Out of guilt, shame, or duty, they do the bare minimum to get by. But true repair goes deeper.

Repairing the wrong is a teaching with a long history in Scripture. In Numbers 5:6-7, God told Moses:

> *When a man or woman commits any sin against another, that person acts unfaithfully toward the Lord and is guilty. The person is to confess the sin he has committed. He is to pay full compensation, add a fifth of its value to it, and give it to the individual he has wronged.*

The Bible tells us to fully compensate for the wrong we have done. But such compensation can be costly to our wallet, to our reputation, and to our pride.

After Tom and Diane began their process of naming their sin against others, individually pursuing those they had wronged, Tom sought to repair what he had done. They were having private conversations with those they had wronged, but Tom also gathered 18 other pastors from the same megachurch and released a joint public statement which named their sin against those who had been fired and slandered. It was an effort to publicly repair the harm that had been done to the reputations of those families. At last, those who had been quietly complicit in the unjust accusations against those elders were loudly correcting the slander they had allowed to continue unchallenged.

It was a big deal for Tom and those other elders to stand up to the megachurch pastor and explicitly name the harm they had all done together. It was also a big deal for Judah to stand up in place of his brother Benjamin.

Repairing the damage to a relationship is not easy. It takes humility and sacrifice. The type of repair shown by Tom and by Judah is only possible because it reflects the deep change of repentance that has gone on in the heart beforehand.

The best motivation to persevere through the humility and vulnerability required to repair the wrong we have done is found in the humility that Jesus took on for us. While Tom and others owed the families of the fired elders this sacrifice, Jesus owed nothing.

He paid back what He had not stolen.
(Belgic Confession, Article 21)

Jesus repaired our relationship with God by paying the debt we could never repay. He made restitution to God in our place. We owed an infinite debt to God for our sinful rebellion. We owed our Creator worship and honor and obedience. But we all got behind on our payments. Like a renter about to be evicted, we had a pile of unpaid bills we could never make up. Our debt to God had accrued interest that only an infinite price could cover. Jesus, the Son of God, made that infinite payment on the cross.

> *He made the one who did not know sin to be sin for us, so that in him we might become the righteousness of God.*
> *(2 Corinthians 5:21)*

God put our debt to himself on Jesus, and in its place, he put Jesus' righteousness over to our accounts. As Christians, we have been reconciled—made right with God. We are also being made righteous as the Spirit transforms us day by day. If we truly comprehend our debt to God and his payment of our sins, and if we truly desire to live in step with the Spirit, then, when it comes to our broken relationship with someone else, we should feel compelled to ask, "How can I *not* make things right?"

Zacchaeus, in Luke 19, must have been familiar with the Old Testament's instructions on repairing wrong in Numbers 5. This Jewish tax collector had long overcharged his countrymen, building his own wealth on dishonest gain. But when he met Jesus, he immediately felt compelled to pay back all he had defrauded—and not just the original amount but four times as much. It was extravagant. But it was also the natural response to seeing his sin clearly and feeling its weight removed from his shoulders by God's mercy and grace through Jesus.

How do we repair the damage we have done? Some situations are simple and obvious. If a little girl has taken a toy from her brother, for example, and she apologizes and receives forgiveness, how does she then make it right? She gives back the toy. Most situations, however, are much more complex!

"

It is hard at times to fathom how to repair what is broken. But how can we not try?

"

Joseph's situation was complex. There are situations in my life and my community that are complex. It is hard at times to fathom how exactly to get to the foundation that is broken under endless layers of cracked walls and floors, sometimes built up over years and even across generations. But, in light of all Christ has done for us, how can we not try?

A SMALL PIECE OF THE PUZZLE

My community in South Carolina has been crippled for years by the lingering legacy of racism and segregation. The year that Desmond Tutu was receiving his Nobel Peace Prize for his anti-violent work to end apartheid in South Africa, I was at a whites-only middle school on the other side of the world. I remember reading my school handbook, which explicitly said that black students could not attend. It didn't sit well with me at the time. It seemed wrong. But everyone I knew thought it was normal. There is something numbing to our own personal consciences in a group that thinks wrong is right and the foolish is ok. Even as a child, I knew something wasn't right. Yet I said nothing.

Finally, in the mid-1980s, the federal government forced my private school to integrate. But the damage was done. Public (state-funded) schools in my community had suffered from the loss of families of means and influence at a crucial time of change. White students like me benefited from the doors opened by our private-school education, while black students were barred from those benefits. The rural area I live in is now known as the Corridor of Shame for its lack of funding for education and the poor results in students' academic performance, all tied to decisions made around integration by those with power and influence in our community.

I grew up in that environment, as did my friends, our parents, and our grandparents. It was the air we breathed. Folks in my community, black and white, seemed to accept that this was just the way things were. But years later, after I moved away to the west coast, I woke up in a cold sweat one day with the knowledge that I had participated in and benefited from the harm done in my community. When I moved back to my hometown, this issue weighed heavily on my mind.

Students of means in our community still mostly attend private schools, which are now open to all. But because I had benefited from something denied to others in my community, I felt convicted that I needed to work in some way to repair that damage. I enrolled my boys in our local public elementary school, one still with very few white students, and started praying about what I might do to repair some of the harm done through the systemic racism I had benefited from.

I now teach developmental math, as a bridge from public schools to college-level mathematics, to students struggling to learn. It's only a small piece of the puzzle in my community, whose education system still bears the fallout of decades of segregation, but it is one piece I am qualified to do. I do not do it as penance. I am not earning my righteousness with God. But God has done so much for me, and he calls me to love my neighbor. I have the ability to contribute in my community in this way. How could I not?

I often wonder, as I drive through the rural farmland in my county, what would have happened if men and women newly freed from slavery had been given the 40 acres and a mule that they were promised at the end of the Civil War? What if folks had received some means to begin to provide for themselves? What if, when schools were integrated, families had worked together to improve education for black and white students in the county? And is there a way, decades later, to repair any of these wrongs? In some cases, apologies have been made, and forgiveness has been offered. But there are no simple ways of making things right.

What can just one woman in one community do? It's simple. I do what I can. I can teach students who missed out on the type of education I had the privilege of receiving. I can support black-owned businesses—doctors, restaurants, insurance agents, and so forth. I can actively listen to friends of color and submit to their opinions about the ways forward. Churches can make sure diverse people are involved at every level of leadership and ministry in the church. White folks can discipline themselves to hear friends' concerns around race and social justice and submit to their input and leadership. None of these things will fully repair the rotten foundation of systemic racism in our country. But all of these things are ways of chipping away at it in our one community at least.

LONG REPAIRS

What does repair look like with the person you wronged? Sometimes it's simple. If you slandered someone publicly, you need to repair their reputation publicly. If you stole from someone, you need to repay them, perhaps with interest. But other situations are harder to figure out. Repairing betrayal in marriage is complex. Repairing the harm done when someone has been unfairly accused or dismissed is complex. Repairing decades of lack of access to education is complex. When the wrong cannot simply be undone, what does repair mean? I don't know your situation, but I encourage you to chip away. Do what you can. You could start by asking the one you wronged what repair would look like to them.

The greatest loss to be repaired is trust. Repairing trust isn't accomplished in a set number of positive interactions. It takes patience. It forces us to face head on the question: do we really value reconciliation with this person enough to persevere through the long process of rebuilding trust? Are we content with spackled cracks in our walls, or do we want a foundation that stands the test of time and pressure?

The patience and sacrifice of repairing the wrongs we have done forces us back to the gospel. We can stay engaged in the process of repairing the wrong we have done because Jesus repaired for us what he had not broken. He repaid our debt to God, which we could never repay ourselves. He then sent us out to repair our relationships with those who have something against us.

Such repair is a priority to Jesus. In the Sermon on the Mount, Jesus told his disciples exactly what to do if someone held something against them. "Leave your gift there in front of the altar," he directed in Matthew 5:24. "First go and be reconciled with your brother or sister, and then come and offer your gift." Before bringing a sacrifice in worship to God, Jesus wanted his disciples to first go to the one they had wronged and repair things with them. Think about that! The worthy response to Jesus' sacrifice for us is, first of all, to turn out toward others and do what we can to be reconciled with them. In light of all Christ has done to reconcile us to God, how can we *not* turn to those we have wronged and offer earthly repair?

> *Therefore, putting away lying, speak the truth, each one to his neighbor, because we are members of one another. … Let the thief no longer steal. Instead, he is to do honest work with his own hands, so that he has something to share with anyone in need. No foul language should come from your mouth, but only what is good for building up someone in need, so that it gives grace to those who hear. And don't grieve God's Holy Spirit. You were sealed by him for the day of redemption. (Ephesians 4:25-30)*

Cracks of Gold

RESTORING THE RELATIONSHIP

After my divorce, as I prepared to move from Seattle to my hometown on the east coast, a dear friend gave me a kintsugi necklace. Kintsugi is a Japanese method for repairing broken pottery. An artisan fills in the cracks of a broken bowl, stone, or glass with a special lacquer mixed with gold. Instead of disguising the injury, it showcases it through the thing that repaired it. The lines that once were cracks become golden art.

God does kintsugi all the time. He puts back the broken parts of our lives in a way that doesn't hide our cracks but allows our brokenness to become a beautiful feature of our story. Our cracks accentuate his grace when the damage is repaired. God invites us to join him in this ministry of reconciliation, showcasing the beauty of his grace as our broken relationships become repaired.

When Judah offered himself in place of Benjamin, God poured golden lacquer into the fissure of Joseph and Judah's relationship. The dam of pent-up emotions immediately broke in Joseph's heart.

> *Joseph could no longer keep his composure in front of all his attendants, so he called out, "Send everyone away from me!" … But he wept so loudly that the Egyptians heard it, and also Pharaoh's household heard it. (Genesis 45:1-2)*

Joseph had previously responded to his brothers with grace, returning their money to them when he sent them home with food the first time, and then hosting them for a meal on their second trip. But that grace was not the same as reconciliation. Now, in light of Judah's sacrificial act signifying his repentance and his desire to repair the damage he had done to his family, Joseph finally revealed himself.

Judah and his brothers weren't just shocked by Joseph's revelation; they were terrified. But Joseph, weeping, bid his brothers come near him. He used a peaceful but pleading word that breaks my heart. "Please," he said, "come near me" (Genesis 45:4). The Hebrew word for "please" here is *na*, a word of entreaty which can also be translated as "I beseech you." Joseph begged his brothers to come close to him. It may seem like a final humiliation for Joseph to be forced to ask the brothers who had cast him away years before to draw close to him once again. But it is a sign of something new. Judah's advocacy for Benjamin had allowed Joseph to risk making himself vulnerable in front of them.

Think of the water that had flowed under the bridge between these brothers! The gulf between them was wide and deep. Yet, with this moment of mutual vulnerability, reconciliation suddenly seemed possible.

A NEW PERSPECTIVE

Joseph's next words to his brothers are stunning.

> *Don't be grieved or angry with yourselves for selling me here, because God sent me ahead of you to preserve life. (v 5)*

Joseph could already see the kintsugi God was doing in his family. For all the pain and humiliation Joseph had suffered, he recognized that he and the rest of his family would be starving to death in Canaan if it hadn't been for the series of events that God had allowed to unfold in Joseph's life.

This was not the perspective Joseph had had in the bowels of the dungeon. For a long time, he had been forced to trust blindly when he could not understand God's plans. But now, Joseph's perspective was like that of a drone flying over the top of his life and his family, surveying the terrain from above. The convoluted path they had taken now made sense. Joseph's tears and struggles had not been wasted. He could see how his story had been fitted together, and why it was good for the long-term stability of his family.

It took years for me to get that perspective on the loss of our church family at the megachurch in Seattle. When I led women's ministry there, I taught hundreds of women at a time. I planned our retreats and teaching events. I discipled in large and small groups. I thought that would be my life's work. I could not envision anything more exciting or fulfilling. When I lost that ministry, I felt it deeply. But after a decade or so, I finally realized that being a deacon in a megachurch and teaching theology to women wasn't the end goal of God's plan for my life.

I had not reached the pinnacle of ministry in my thirties. I would not be spending the last decades of my life longing for the past. I recognize now that I was learning lessons from what I had experienced in that megachurch—both the good and the bad—so that I could better minister where I am now. God was preparing me all along for ministry in my small multicultural church plant. I am now able to look at my life from the perspective of a drone hovering above it all, and I can make sense of the turns that only seemed chaotic and destructive at the time.

"

The convoluted path they had taken now made sense. Joseph's tears and struggles had not been wasted.

"

But many of us have not been gifted with such perspective on the hard roads we have walked—at least not yet. I spent years after the megachurch conflict feeling all that was wrong with the world. That conflict didn't represent God's kingdom coming. It didn't give testimony to the gospel. It didn't show our church loving God with all our heart or our neighbor as ourselves. If I'd tried to apply Joseph's words to my own life then, they would have felt offensive. "Don't be grieved or angry with yourselves." When you are waiting for someone to finally acknowledge their sin against you, those words feel dismissive. Perhaps you still bear scars from deep harm done to you. Does it feel as if Joseph was offering cheap grace to his brothers? Was he minimizing the brothers' sins against him? *It's ok, guys. God had a plan, and you don't need to worry about all the harm you did.*

Remember that Judah had just offered his life in place of Benjamin's. Joseph knew, from overhearing his brothers' conversations on their first trip to Egypt, that they felt great guilt for the wrong they had done to him. They were painfully aware of what they deserved for their sin against Joseph and their father. Judah, in particular, knew that his life was the just payment for his sins, and he had shown himself to be willing to pay it! Judah's genuine change of heart and the actions that proved it were what had made Joseph's words possible. The brothers had already faced head on the horror of their harm toward Joseph and their father. Joseph was not offering cheap grace.

After his hurried explanation to ease his brothers' shock and terror, Joseph threw his arms around Benjamin, who wept on his shoulder. Joseph, still weeping, then kissed each of his brothers. "Afterward," says the author of Genesis, "his brothers talked with him" (v 15).

That last sentence gives me pause. After the terror and weeping described in the previous verses, it seems that emotions were calmed and a new kind of fellowship and communication started. Had these brothers ever just talked before? It is the first conversation we read of in Genesis that doesn't involve bitter jealousy or fear between them. What an amazing moment for these brothers: a moment that started them down an entirely new path. Golden lacquer was poured into the broken crevices of their relationship, and we see it rejoining their fractured family. Things would be different than before—still scarred—but beautiful nonetheless. If you have not yet experienced any reconciliation with the one who harmed you or the one you harmed, let this conversation between Joseph and his brothers whet your appetite for what is possible through God's supernatural grace.

THE FATHER'S EMBRACE

When Jacob heard the news about Joseph, he was stunned. He had been deflated when circumstances forced him to send Benjamin with his brothers to Egypt. "If I am deprived of my sons, then I am deprived" (Genesis 43:14). But when he learned that, far from losing all his sons, he had regained the one he had given up for dead, his spirit revived (45:27). His dull eyes regained some clarity. His stooped shoulders widened and straightened. I imagine this hunched old man standing a little taller as an energy buzzed in him that he had not felt in decades.

At Joseph's invitation, the entire family headed to Egypt. God assured Jacob that, though his family was leaving their promised homeland, God would one day bring them back. The family made its way to the land Pharaoh was giving them, but Joseph didn't wait for his father to make it all the way before he rushed out in his chariot to meet him.

Joseph presented himself to him, threw his arms around him, and wept for a long time. (Genesis 46:29)

What was that moment like for Joseph? His father had been his protector in youth. But now he was old and frail. What did his bones and tissue feel like in Joseph's arms? Joseph leaned against him, finally resting in the arms of his father.

What was this moment like for Jacob? His teenage son was now a grown man. What did his tall, fully grown body feel like against Jacob's? Did Jacob feel his frailty against his son's strength? His empty arms were full again. His son was a man of power, physically and socially.

Pharaoh welcomed Jacob and his family into Egypt. He gave them a place to live in Goshen, in the delta of the Nile River. Joseph was physically reconciled with his family. He was no longer a slave living far from them. It seems that the story is complete.

But the story of this family conflict and resolution has an important addendum. This embrace of Joseph and Jacob was not the final chapter. Nor was Pharaoh's welcome of the family into the land. They had been reconciled physically, but there was a final scene of repentance and repair still to take place between Joseph and the brothers who sold him into slavery.

RE-REPENTING

For 17 years, Jacob lived with his reunited family in Egypt. His sons, daughters, grandsons, and granddaughters all dwelled safely there under the protection of Joseph. But Jacob eventually grew weaker. As he lay dying, he called his sons to himself. He used his last energy to tell them of their future inheritance. Joseph's sons, Manasseh and Ephraim, would receive a double blessing, each becoming the heads of a tribe of Israel along with their uncles. Then, nearly two decades after Jacob and all of his family moved to Egypt, 40 or so years after Joseph had first been sold into slavery, Jacob died.

Joseph grieved his father's death deeply. The family mourned for months in Egypt before Joseph and his brothers finally took their father's body back to Canaan to fulfill his wish to be buried with his people.

At this point, years after Judah had seemed to genuinely repent to Joseph, the brothers approached Joseph a second time.

> *They said to one another, "If Joseph is holding a grudge against us, he will certainly repay us for all the suffering we caused him." So they sent this message to Joseph, "Before he died your father gave a command: 'Say this to Joseph: Please forgive your brothers' transgression and their sin—the suffering they caused you.' Therefore, please forgive the transgression of the servants of the God of your father." Joseph wept when their message came to him. His brothers also came to him, bowed down before him, and said, "We are your slaves!" (Genesis 50:15-18)*

I am struck by several questions as I read this interaction between Joseph and his brothers. What kind of relationship had they had for the 17 years they had lived together in Egypt? Did Joseph's position as Pharaoh's second-in-command keep him separate from them? Judah had had a genuinely repentant interaction with Joseph after Benjamin was found with Joseph's silver cup, but maybe the other brothers hadn't repented. Was this the first time that Reuben, Simeon, Levi, and the rest had clearly articulated to Joseph's face exactly how they had sinned against him? Was this the first time they had specifically asked for forgiveness?

Most of all, I wonder about the brothers' motives. Verse 15 shows they were clearly fearful of possible retribution from Joseph after their father died. Were they also motivated by genuine sorrow about how they had harmed Joseph? Were they telling the truth when they said that Jacob had instructed them to say these things to Joseph? Or were they using their father's death to manipulate Joseph into releasing them from any penalty for the harm they had done to him so long before?

I do not know the answers to these questions. But one thing remains clear through this final recorded conversation between Joseph and his brothers. Their path to reconciliation was not a tidy, linear progression. Most likely, yours won't be either.

As you read of Joseph's convoluted path to reconciliation with his brothers, what path is your own reconciliation of broken relationships taking? Do you long to hear the words "I forgive you"? Or do you struggle to say them? Have you forgiven someone who does not acknowledge the harm they have done? Maybe you have released them from their control over you, but reconciliation remains far off. Have you acknowledged the harm you have done to another and repaired it in the ways you can? Does reconciliation seem to be on the horizon for you and the one you harmed? Or are you and your loved one still spackling over cracks in the walls, unwilling or unable to dig to the deeper foundation?

It is scary to contemplate going to that deeper level, and sometimes we have no idea even how to try. The risks of emotional vulnerability may seem to outweigh the estrangement we feel in the present. In those cases, we must pray. We need God's supernatural help to make it over hurdles too high for ourselves. But, as my friend Esther often tells our church family, God is able and kind. Do not lose hope. Reconciliation is possible.

In this scene in Genesis 50, Joseph's brothers at first didn't sound as if they were repenting at all. *Your father commanded you to forgive us.* But by the end of their conversation, the brothers had humbled themselves before Joseph. "We are your slaves," they said (v 18). They deserved to be punished for what they had done to Joseph. Imprisonment would have been the just penalty for their sin. This seems to me to be a repetition of the process Judah had gone through years before. From selling Joseph into slavery to offering themselves as Joseph's slaves, these brothers faced head on exactly what they had done and acknowledged that it was wrong.

Joseph's response to them is iconic, but, like his words to Judah in 45:5, it may vex those who have been sinned against.

> *"Don't be afraid. Am I in the place of God? You planned evil against me; God planned it for good to bring about the present result—the survival of many people. Therefore don't be afraid. I will take care of you and your children." And he comforted them and spoke kindly to them.*
> *(Genesis 50:19-21)*

Have you been confronted with this passage in an attempt to pressure you to forgive? Genesis 50:20 gets used out of context at times, and context matters in Scripture. We misuse Joseph's response when we remove it from the context of the previous 40 years of history between Joseph and his brothers, including their very specific words of confession and repentance that were uttered in verses 16-18. In the years since Joseph first saw his brothers in person in Egypt, they had confessed the wrong they had done to him, they had repented of their wrongdoing, and they had repaired the wrong in the ways that they were able to. In the context of this long history, Joseph's response is beautiful and hopeful.

Sin had bombed Joseph's life, but God had sovereignly guided the fallout. He would keep his promises to Jacob's family and use the deep pain Joseph's brothers had caused to make the fulfillment of those promises even more resplendent. If Joseph's family was a broken piece of pottery, shattered by his brothers' sin against him, Joseph saw them now through the beauty of the golden repairs God had done to bring them back together.

"Don't be afraid," he encouraged his brothers. Promising to take care of them and their children, he spoke kindly to them. He comforted them. The last phrase of verse 21 could also be translated, "He spoke to their hearts." This broken family had taken a convoluted path over nearly 50 years, from Joseph's first dream of his brothers bowing down to him to this last moment of reconciliation when they actually did so. Now Joseph looked his brothers in their eyes and spoke to their hearts. He assured them that he would not turn against them. He assured them that they and their children were safe. He enabled them to enter their own old age at peace.

Jacob's family walked a complex path to reconciliation—a path that turned back on itself at enough points to be discouraging. This final scene of re-repenting gives me hope. When our own path to reconciliation seems to stall, or the steps we take don't seem to accomplish what we expected, we are not at the end. If you made yourself vulnerable to the one you harmed and they did not respond as you hoped, your road to reconciliation is not over. If you have forgiven the one who wronged you but they still can't name their sin against you, your road to reconciliation isn't at its end either. We have hope that God, in his time, will do the work in hearts that we cannot do ourselves.

Your job may be to name your sin specifically to the one you harmed and seek to repair the damage in the ways you can. Or your job may be to forgive your offender, releasing them of their need to repay their debt to you. God oversees both. He alone can pour the golden lacquer of reconciliation into broken relationships and make them into a beautiful new work of art. If you are still waiting for such reconciliation, then wait in peace, confident in God's kindness and in his ability to see this process to the end.

Listen to me, house of Jacob,
all the remnant of the house of Israel,
who have been sustained from the womb,
carried along since birth.
I will be the same until your old age,
and I will bear you up when you turn gray.
I have made you, and I will carry you;
I will bear and rescue you. (Isaiah 46:3-4)

Conclusion

"I forgive you."

As we reach the end of this book, what do these words mean to you? Are these the words you still long to hear? Are they the words you still struggle to say? Maybe they are the words you have heard but can't quite believe or the words you've said but still battle to really mean.

Angela, the wife of one of the elders fired all those years ago, recently talked with me about the twisted path we have both taken to forgiveness and reconciliation in our broken relationships with others from that megachurch. At times, it seemed we would never get to reconciliation with those who had wronged us. I asked her point blank if she felt she had truly reconciled with anyone core to that church conflict. "Absolutely," she replied. Our conversation encouraged me because, even after bitter betrayal, several sweet relationships I did not know about had been restored. It was harder to reach that point with some who had harmed her than others, she admitted, and all of the relationships still showed their kintsugi cracks. Relationships were repaired, but the scarring from the break was now part of their new form.

Angela and I also talked about those in that church conflict who had not named their sins—the ones who had not attempted to repair the harm they had participated in. I talked with Paul, the other elder who had been fired and slandered, about the same problem. I asked if he could forgive those who had never acknowledged the harm they had done to him and his family. He replied simply with Jesus' words on the cross: "Father, forgive them, because they do not know what they are doing" (Luke 23:34).

The families of the Charleston Nine spoke words of forgiveness to a man who had shown no remorse over anything he had done. Jesus did too.

Wherever you are in this journey, you cannot make others recognize their sins against you. We cannot force someone to confess their sins or repair the wrong they have done. We certainly cannot force repentance, which is a work of God's kindness in the heart of the sinner. However, there is one place that you and I can certainly get to on the convoluted path of reconciliation. We can forgive. The words "I forgive you" are not synonymous with reconciliation with the one who wronged you. But those words do equip you for peace within yourself in a way that little else can.

To forgive is not to sweep sin under the carpet. It is not downplaying the harm that was done. Neither does forgiveness mean we leave an unrepentant offender free to harm others in the future as they have in the past. It does mean we choose to see the humanity of the offender and hope for their repentance. It means we leave vengeance to God. It means we release the one who wronged us from their role as offender in our life. It means we forgive their debt as Christ has forgiven ours.

To do this, we must lean into a longer story, an eternal one, that gives us the perspective we need to respond to unreconciled earthly stories with hope.

THE FINAL SCENE

The young man forced against his will into servitude in Egypt rested as an old man in a home second only to the quarters of Pharaoh. He had provided for his nation. He had provided for his family. But now his own breathing was labored. He could tell his days were coming to an end. His children, grandchildren, and great-grandchildren gathered around him, along with his remaining brothers.

Joseph had lived surrounded by his beloved family for decades now. But he was still alienated from his homeland. Years before, God met Jacob on his way to see Joseph and promised:

I will go down with you to Egypt, and I will also bring you back. (Genesis 46:4)

Jacob believed God's promise, and so did Joseph. As Joseph breathed his last breaths, he made his brothers and children promise that they would take him home with them when they returned to their homeland, even if he was just a pile of bones in a box. Joseph believed God's promises to his family—even those he wouldn't live to see fulfilled.

By the time the people of Israel finally returned to the promised land, Joseph's brothers and children had passed away. But his request was honored by the generation that left Egypt with Moses.

Moses took the bones of Joseph with him, because Joseph had made the Israelites swear a solemn oath, saying, "God will certainly come to your aid; then you must take my bones with you from this place." (Exodus 13:19)

The book of Hebrews gives the final word on Joseph's legacy in Scripture. Hebrews 11 speaks of the faith of individuals in the history of Israel. Joseph, for all the lessons in his life as he navigated the sins against him, isn't affirmed in Hebrews for forgiving his brothers or for faithfulness to his family but for the final instructions he gave to take his bones to the promised land.

> *By faith Isaac blessed Jacob and Esau concerning things to come. By faith Jacob, when he was dying, blessed each of the sons of Joseph ... By faith Joseph, as he was nearing the end of his life, mentioned the exodus of the Israelites and gave instructions concerning his bones. (Hebrews 11:20-22)*

Isaac believed in the things to come and blessed his sons in light of a future he did not get to experience in his own lifetime. Jacob did too. And Joseph, on his deathbed, believed that God was going to finish what he had promised to Joseph's father and grandfather. Joseph believed God was going to bring his family back home. His confidence in God's larger plans was also the supernatural motivation for his extraordinary grace and mercy to his brothers, who had wronged him so deeply. They meant it for evil, but God meant it for good. We already know how God had used it for good during Joseph's lifetime—but God also ultimately had a long plan for Joseph's family that transcended Joseph's lifetime. God planned to save the world through One born of Jacob's family: one descended from Judah. Joseph didn't fully understand that at the time, but he did believe that God was doing something bigger the events of his own life. That was what gave him the perspective he needed to co-operate with the greater good God was working—a greater good in which Joseph's vengeance could have no role.

If we only have hope in this life, the apostle Paul said in 1 Corinthians 15:19, we should be pitied. God is doing something bigger than our lives that gives perspective to our lives. He is doing something bigger that equips us to confess our sins, to repent of our wrongdoing, to forgive those who have wronged us, and to repair the wrong we have done.

"

God is doing something
bigger than our lives. He
is building something
eternally good.

"

He is building his church, his body. He is calling people to himself and radically changing their lives. He is reconciling people left and right, reconciling them to himself and reconciling them to each other as he builds his kingdom in and through us. Nothing can overcome this work. He will accomplish it.

I will build my church, and the gates of Hades will not overpower it. (Matthew 16:18)

All of us in Christ are part of something eternal, even as God works right now in our immediate circumstances. He will redeem all that is wrong in the world and make it right in his new and beautiful kingdom. Such belief in something bigger equipped Tom and Diane to repent and the families of the Charleston Nine to forgive. Such belief in God's larger plan equipped Joseph to forgive and be reconciled with his brothers. And such belief has equipped me to find new footing after my divorce and to trust in God's good plan for my family. Confidence in Christ's good plan for us for eternity equips each of us to forgive as well. It gives us a different perspective on all we face in this world and confident hope for full justice and reconciliation—if not in this life, then certainly in the next.

We can confess our sins because we believe God is doing something bigger in our lives and eternal outside of our lives. We can repair the wrong we have done because we believe God is building something eternally good in which our kintsugi offerings adorn the walls. And we can forgive those who have wronged us because before time began, God put a plan in motion to forgive us. We believe in something bigger than ourselves; we can confidently hope in God to bring it all to pass. Christ bore our debts on the cross in our place, and his eternal work for us equips us to forgive and be forgiven.

He himself bore our sins in his body on the tree; so that, having died to sins, we might live for righteousness. By his wounds you have been healed. (1 Peter 2:24)

You planned evil against me; God planned it for good.
(Genesis 50:20)

the good book

COMPANY

BIBLICAL | RELEVANT | ACCESSIBLE

At The Good Book Company, we are dedicated to helping Christians and local churches grow. We believe that God's growth process always starts with hearing clearly what he has said to us through his timeless word—the Bible.

Ever since we opened our doors in 1991, we have been striving to produce Bible-based resources that bring glory to God. We have grown to become an international provider of user-friendly resources to the Christian community, with believers of all backgrounds and denominations using our books, Bible studies, devotionals, evangelistic resources, and DVD-based courses.

We want to equip ordinary Christians to live for Christ day by day, and churches to grow in their knowledge of God, their love for one another, and the effectiveness of their outreach.

Call us for a discussion of your needs or visit one of our local websites for more information on the resources and services we provide.

Your friends at The Good Book Company

thegoodbook.com | thegoodbook.co.uk
thegoodbook.com.au | thegoodbook.co.nz
thegoodbook.co.in